MAJOR WORLD LEADERS

YASIR ARAFAT

MENACHEM BEGIN

TONY BLAIR

GEORGE W. BUSH

JIMMY CARTER

VICENTE FOX

SADDAM HUSSEIN

HOSNI MUBARAK

VLADIMIR PUTIN

MOHAMMED REZA PAHLAVI

ANWAR SADAT

THE SAUDI ROYAL FAMILY

The Saudi Royal Family

Jennifer Bond Reed

CHELSEA HOUSE
PUBLISHERS
A Haights Cross Communications Company

Philadelphia

CHELSEA HOUSE PUBLISHERS

EDITOR IN CHIEF Sally Cheney
DIRECTOR OF PRODUCTION Kim Shinners
CREATIVE MANAGER Takeshi Takahashi
MANUFACTURING MANAGER Diann Grasse

Staff for THE SAUDI ROYAL FAMILY

EDITOR Lee Marcott
ASSOCIATE EDITOR Patrick Stone
PRODUCTION ASSISTANT Jaimie Winkler
PICTURE RESEARCH 21st Century Publishing and Communications, Inc.
SERIES DESIGNER Takeshi Takahashi
COVER DESIGNER Keith Trego
LAYOUT 21st Century Publishing and Communications, Inc.

A Haights Cross Communications ✦ Company

http://www.chelseahouse.com

First Printing

1 3 5 7 9 8 6 4 2

Library of Congress Cataloging-in-Publication Data applied for.

Reed, Jennifer.
  The Saudi royal family / Jennifer Bond Reed.
    v. cm.—(Major world leaders)
Includes bibliographical references and index.
Contents: Humble origins—Desert kingdom—King Abdul Aziz: a new kingdom—King Saud, the black sheikh: 1953–1964—King Faisal, the hero: 1964–1975—King Khalid, the quiet one: 1975–1982—King Fahd—Friend or foe: the future of Saudi Arabia.
    ISBN 0-7910-7063-8 — ISBN 0-7910-7187-1 (pbk.)
  1. Saudi Arabia—Kings and rulers—Biography—Juvenile literature. [1. Saudi Arabia—Kings and rulers. 2. Saudi Arabia—History. 3. Kings, queens, rulers, etc.] I. Title. II. Series.
DS204.25 .R44 2002
953.8'009'9—dc21
                                                                2002007455

TABLE OF CONTENTS

On Leadership

Arthur M. Schlesinger, jr.

Leadership, it may be said, is really what makes the world go round. Love no doubt smoothes the passage; but love is a private transaction between consenting adults. Leadership is a public transaction with history. The idea of leadership affirms the capacity of individuals to move, inspire, and mobilize masses of people so that they act together in pursuit of an end. Sometimes leadership serves good purposes, sometimes bad; but whether the end is benign or evil, great leaders are those men and women who leave their personal stamp on history.

Now, the very concept of leadership implies the proposition that individuals can make a difference. This proposition has never been universally accepted. From classical times to the present day, eminent thinkers have regarded individuals as no more than the agents and pawns of larger forces, whether the gods and goddesses of the ancient world or, in the modern era, race, class, nation, the dialectic, the will of the people, the spirit of the times, history itself. Against such forces, the individual dwindles into insignificance.

So contends the thesis of historical determinism. Tolstoy's great novel *War and Peace* offers a famous statement of the case. Why, Tolstoy asked, did millions of men in the Napoleonic Wars, denying their human feelings and their common sense, move back and forth across Europe slaughtering their fellows? "The war," Tolstoy answered, "was bound to happen simply because it was bound to happen." All prior history determined it. As for leaders, they, Tolstoy said, "are but the labels that serve to give a name to an end and, like labels, they have the least possible connection with the event." The greater the leader, "the more conspicuous the inevitability and the predestination of every act he commits." The leader, said Tolstoy, is "the slave of history."

Determinism takes many forms. Marxism is the determinism of class. Nazism the determinism of race. But the idea of men and women as the slaves of history runs athwart the deepest human instincts. Rigid determinism abolishes the idea of human freedom—the assumption of free choice that underlies every move we make, every word we speak, every thought we think. It abolishes the idea of human responsibility, since it is manifestly unfair to reward or punish people for actions that are by definition beyond their control. No one can live consistently by any deterministic creed. The Marxist states prove this themselves by their extreme susceptibility to the cult of leadership.

More than that, history refutes the idea that individuals make no difference. In December 1931 a British politician crossing Fifth Avenue in New York City between 76th and 77th Streets around 10:30 P.M. looked in the wrong direction and was knocked down by an automobile—a moment, he later recalled, of a man aghast, a world aglare: "I do not understand why I was not broken like an eggshell or squashed like a gooseberry." Fourteen months later an American politician, sitting in an open car in Miami, Florida, was fired on by an assassin; the man beside him was hit. Those who believe that individuals make no difference to history might well ponder whether the next two decades would have been the same had Mario Constasino's car killed Winston Churchill in 1931 and Giuseppe Zangara's bullet killed Franklin Roosevelt in 1933. Suppose, in addition, that Lenin had died of typhus in Siberia in 1895 and that Hitler had been killed on the western front in 1916. What would the 20th century have looked like now?

For better or for worse, individuals do make a difference. "The notion that a people can run itself and its affairs anonymously," wrote the philosopher William James, "is now well known to be the silliest of absurdities. Mankind does nothing save through initiatives on the part of inventors, great or small, and imitation by the rest of us—these are the sole factors in human progress. Individuals of genius show the way, and set the patterns, which common people then adopt and follow."

Leadership, James suggests, means leadership in thought as well as in action. In the long run, leaders in thought may well make the greater difference to the world. "The ideas of economists and political philosophers, both when they are right and when they are wrong," wrote John Maynard Keynes, "are more powerful than is commonly understood. Indeed the world is ruled by little else. Practical men, who believe themselves to be quite exempt from any intellectual influences, are usually the slaves of some defunct economist. . . . The power of vested interests is vastly exaggerated compared with the gradual encroachment of ideas."

But, as Woodrow Wilson once said, "Those only are leaders of men, in the general eye, who lead in action. . . . It is at their hands that new thought gets its translation into the crude language of deeds." Leaders in thought often invent in solitude and obscurity, leaving to later generations the tasks of imitation. Leaders in action—the leaders portrayed in this series—have to be effective in their own time.

And they cannot be effective by themselves. They must act in response to the rhythms of their age. Their genius must be adapted, in a phrase from William James, "to the receptivities of the moment." Leaders are useless without followers. "There goes the mob," said the French politician, hearing a clamor in the streets. "I am their leader. I must follow them." Great leaders turn the inchoate emotions of the mob to purposes of their own. They seize on the opportunities of their time, the hopes, fears, frustrations, crises, potentialities. They succeed when events have prepared the way for them, when the community is awaiting to be aroused, when they can provide the clarifying and organizing ideas. Leadership completes the circuit between the individual and the mass and thereby alters history.

It may alter history for better or for worse. Leaders have been responsible for the most extravagant follies and most monstrous crimes that have beset suffering humanity. They have also been vital in such gains as humanity has made in individual freedom, religious and racial tolerance, social justice, and respect for human rights.

There is no sure way to tell in advance who is going to lead for good and who for evil. But a glance at the gallery of men and women in MAJOR WORLD LEADERS suggests some useful tests.

One test is this: Do leaders lead by force or by persuasion? By command or by consent? Through most of history leadership was exercised by the divine right of authority. The duty of followers was to defer and to obey. "Theirs not to reason why/Theirs but to do and die." On occasion, as with the so-called enlightened despots of the 18th century in Europe, absolutist leadership was animated by humane purposes. More often, absolutism nourished the passion for domination, land, gold, and conquest and resulted in tyranny.

The great revolution of modern times has been the revolution of equality. "Perhaps no form of government," wrote the British historian James Bryce in his study of the United States, *The American Commonwealth*, "needs great leaders so much as democracy." The idea that all people should be equal in their legal condition has undermined the old structure of authority, hierarchy, and deference. The revolution of equality has had two contrary effects on the nature of leadership. For equality, as Alexis de Tocqueville pointed out in his great study *Democracy in America*, might mean equality in servitude as well as equality in freedom.

"I know of only two methods of establishing equality in the political world," Tocqueville wrote. "Rights must be given to every citizen, or none at all to anyone . . . save one, who is the master of all." There was no middle ground "between the sovereignty of all and the absolute power of one man." In his astonishing prediction of 20th-century totalitarian dictatorship, Tocqueville explained how the revolution of equality could lead to the *Führerprinzip* and more terrible absolutism than the world had ever known.

But when rights are given to every citizen and the sovereignty of all is established, the problem of leadership takes a new form, becomes more exacting than ever before. It is easy to issue commands and enforce them by the rope and the stake, the concentration camp and the *gulag*. It is much harder to use argument and achievement to overcome opposition and win consent. The Founding Fathers of the United States understood the difficulty. They believed that history had given them the opportunity to decide, as Alexander Hamilton wrote in the first Federalist Paper, whether men are indeed capable of basing government on "reflection and choice, or whether they are forever destined to depend . . . on accident and force."

Government by reflection and choice called for a new style of leadership and a new quality of followership. It required leaders to be responsive to popular concerns, and it required followers to be active and informed participants in the process. Democracy does not eliminate emotion from politics; sometimes it fosters demagoguery; but it is confident that, as the greatest of democratic leaders put it, you cannot fool all of the people all of the time. It measures leadership by results and retires those who overreach or falter or fail.

It is true that in the long run despots are measured by results too. But they can postpone the day of judgment, sometimes indefinitely, and in the meantime they can do infinite harm. It is also true that democracy is no guarantee of virtue and intelligence in government, for the voice of the people is not necessarily the voice of God. But democracy, by assuring the right of opposition, offers built-in resistance to the evils inherent in absolutism. As the theologian Reinhold Niebuhr summed it up, "Man's capacity for justice makes democracy possible, but man's inclination to justice makes democracy necessary."

A second test for leadership is the end for which power is sought. When leaders have as their goal the supremacy of a master race or the promotion of totalitarian revolution or the acquisition and exploitation of colonies or the protection of greed and privilege or the preservation of personal power, it is likely that their leadership will do little to advance the cause of humanity. When their goal is the abolition of slavery, the liberation of women, the enlargement of opportunity for the poor and powerless, the extension of equal rights to racial minorities, the defense of the freedoms of expression and opposition, it is likely that their leadership will increase the sum of human liberty and welfare.

Leaders have done great harm to the world. They have also conferred great benefits. You will find both sorts in this series. Even "good" leaders must be regarded with a certain wariness. Leaders are not demigods; they put on their trousers one leg after another just like ordinary mortals. No leader is infallible, and every leader needs to be reminded of this at regular intervals. Irreverence irritates leaders but is their salvation. Unquestioning submission corrupts leaders and demeans followers. Making a cult of a leader is always a mistake. Fortunately hero worship generates its own antidote. "Every hero," said Emerson, "becomes a bore at last."

The signal benefit the great leaders confer is to embolden the rest of us to live according to our own best selves, to be active, insistent, and resolute in affirming our own sense of things. For great leaders attest to the reality of human freedom against the supposed inevitabilities of history. And they attest to the wisdom and power that may lie within the most unlikely of us, which is why Abraham Lincoln remains the supreme example of great leadership. A great leader, said Emerson, exhibits new possibilities to all humanity. "We feed on genius . . . . Great men exist that there may be greater men."

Great leaders, in short, justify themselves by emancipating and empowering their followers. So humanity struggles to master its destiny, remembering with Alexis de Tocqueville: "It is true that around every man a fatal circle is traced beyond which he cannot pass; but within the wide verge of that circle he is powerful and free; as it is with man, so with communities." ■

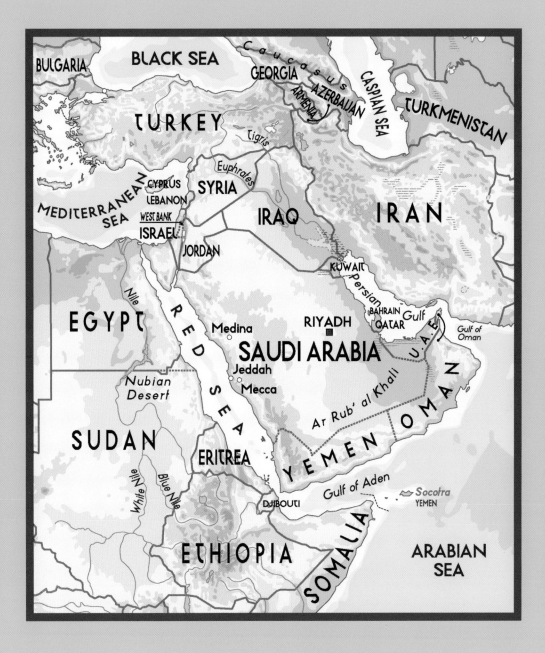

Portraits of King Fahd and the Saudi kings who ruled before him look down on Saudi subjects waiting in National Guard headquarters in Riyadh, Saudi Arabia's capital city.

Humble Origins

The country of Saudi Arabia is rich in tradition. Society follows the strict guidelines and rules of the Koran, the holy book of the Islamic religion. Everything is based on the Koran: what the children learn in school, how the women dress, how the men should behave and act. It has been this way for many hundreds of years, and it continues to be the way for Saudi nationals in the 21st century.

Saudi Arabia has isolated itself from the rest of the world, but the rest of the world is slowly creeping into Saudi society. In particular, the values and customs of the West are influencing many newly wealthy Saudi people, including the Saudi royal family, whose members are free to leave the country and return as they please. Seeing the freedom enjoyed by the rest of the world, it is difficult not to want the same thing. Yet such freedom is at odds with their religion and way of life.

The once desolate area known today as Saudi Arabia is home to one of the wealthiest families, possibly the wealthiest family, in the world—the Al Saud. Now the ruling family of Saudi Arabia, only a few hundred years ago they were poor farmers. In only a brief period of time in our world history, they gained complete control over the entire country and found a new form of wealth: oil. Their wealth is so new, in fact, that they hardly know how to handle it in a responsible, beneficial way.

The Al Saud family comes from humble beginnings and the rulers of today try hard not to forget their ancestry, but living in a modern world and wondering what to do with their fortunes can cause serious problems. The religion of Islam teaches them to live one way, yet money shows them another. The Western media and even Saudi's own citizens constantly ridicule members of the Al Saud family for their lavish spending, and with reason. Due in large part to their spending, both the economy of Saudi Arabia and the general well-being of many Saudi citizens have improved greatly over the last thirty years. Hospitals and schools have been built. Modern buildings now outnumber the adobe structures that once made up the entire city of Riyadh. Streets are paved, and the infrastructure of many cities is greatly improved. Military strength has increased. But despite all this benevolence, corruption has also seeped into the lives of many members of the royal family.

Where did the power and money come from, and what is the future of the royal family of Saudi Arabia? The answer to these questions lies in the past. To understand the Al Saud family, we must look at its origins.

THE PROPHET MUHAMMAD

Faith—belief in Allah, the god of Islam—is the most important thing in a true Muslim's life. Nothing, not even money or power, compares to a Muslim's relationship with God. Islam dominates not just Saudi society, but that of much of the Middle East. Just like the royal family of Saudi Arabia, however, Islam's origin is humble and elusive.

Unless you are a Muslim or an Islamic scholar, you may not know about Muhammad and how he influenced the development of the Islamic religion. Surprisingly, he derived some of what he taught from a Christian monk and the Hebrew religion.

Near the end of the 6th century of the Christian era—for Muslims do not follow the Western calendar, which is based on the birth of Christ—a boy was born in Mecca, a huge trading city and caravan oasis that drew people from all over the Middle East, people of many different beliefs and ways of life. At this time, the people of Mecca worshiped many gods. They did not believe that there was just one god, as the prophets of the Old and New Testaments taught. The Christians and Jews of the time both believed in the Old Testament, which makes up the first half of the Christian Bible today.

When Muhammad was six years old, his parents died and he went to live with his uncle, who was a merchant. His new family expected Muhammad to learn from his uncle and become a merchant as well, and to work with his uncle when he came of age.

Being a merchant did not mean simply setting up shop and selling products. Merchants traveled in caravans and sold their goods all over the peninsula of Arabia. This was a very dangerous job. Bedouins often raided the caravans, killing the merchants and stealing their goods. Bedouins were nomadic herders who saw the caravans as an easy source of food and the other products they needed to live in their hostile environment. Raiding caravans was part of their way of life for hundreds of years. It was also an inevitable part of life for merchants. Muhammad probably learned about desert warfare while traveling the dangerous caravan routes.

Muhammad met a Christian monk named Bahira, who

considered Muhammad gifted, despite his wild demeanor and lack of education. Bahira failed to convert Muhammad to Christianity, but the impact he made on Muhammad lasted a lifetime. He did convince Muhammad that there was only one god and taught him about the great prophets of the Old Testament—prophets such as Abraham, Moses, and Solomon, who are still important to Muslims today.

Soon after Muhammad turned forty, he became deeply depressed. He could no longer bear the injustices he continually saw around him: poverty, homelessness, brutality, and inequality. Muhammad felt that these injustices were the price society paid for its pagan beliefs. He left the merchant trade and spent his days praying in a nearby cave. One day, during his prayers, he felt his chest constrict and found it difficult to breathe. As he struggled for breath, he made a guttural sound: *qur'an.* This is now the name of the central religious text of Islam—the Koran—and means "to read or recite."

Muhammad had divine revelations for some time, and believed the angel Gabriel sent messages to him from God. These messages revealed the Word of God, which became the Koran, the holy book of Islam.

At first, Muhammad was unsure of his calling. Converting people who believed in many gods to a belief in one god was difficult. Most of Muhammad's family shunned him, although his wife supported him and believed he was truly a messenger for God. Despite numerous plots against his life by those who adhered to pagan beliefs, Muhammad refused to give up his faith. He expanded his message into lessons on brotherhood and the equality of man. He taught that slaves were equal to their masters and the lower class was equal to the upper class. This was welcome news to slaves, but many slave owners and members of the upper class didn't condone Muhammad's teachings.

When he could no longer bear the injustices he saw around him in 6th-century Arabia, the Prophet Muhammad left his life as a caravan trader and retreated to a desert cave called Hira. This engraving depicts Muhammad praying for guidance from the Muslim god, Allah.

More than two million Muslim pilgrims from around the world travel to Mecca on a pilgrimage called the *hajj*. Here, thousands perform evening prayers inside the Grand Mosque, Islam's holiest shrine. The black cube in the upper right is the *Kaaba* or *Ka'ba*, which, in the Islamic religious tradition, God commanded Abraham to build 4,000 years ago. According to doctrine, God then told Abraham to summon all mankind to visit the shrine. Today, Islam is the fastest-growing religion in the world.

Despite constant threats against his life, Muhammad accepted an invitation to the city of Medina to help bring peace to two warring tribes. His journey between Mecca and Medina in A.D. 622 has since become the most important journey in Islam. It is called the *Hegira* and literally means "flight." The

Hegira marked the beginning of the Islamic calendar and perhaps the beginning of Islam itself.

Once in Medina, Muhammad calmed the rivalry between the two tribes. He also met with a group of people who believed in one god, the Jews. Through this interaction, Muhammad adopted many Jewish customs and traditions into his own religion. For example, he set aside a Sabbath or Holy Day. He taught Muslims to face Jerusalem when they prayed, and he insisted on three obligatory prayers. However, when the more educated Jews of the time ridiculed Muhammad for his lack of education and poor knowledge of the Old Testament, Muhammad broke his ties with the Jews. He changed the Sabbath day to Friday and urged all Muslims to face Mecca when praying. He also began a month of fasting, called *Ramadan*, and the *hajj*, the pilgrimage to Mecca.

He became known as a conqueror and reformer, but he is best known as a messenger of God on Earth. Muhammad died in A.D. 632, but today Islam, the religion he founded, is the most rapidly growing religion in the world.

MUHAMMAD BIN ABD AL-WAHHAB AND THE BIRTH OF THE WAHHABI SECT

The religion of Islam founded by Muhammad became the sole religion of Arabia. Today it's the way of life, the very essence of Saudi society. However, Arabia was a divided country.

Just as Protestants and Catholics have fought for centuries in the name of Christ, the Sunnis and Shiites have fought for centuries in the name of Muhammad. Hostilities between the Sunnis and Shiites date back to the years after Muhammad's death. Both believe in Islam, but the two groups followed different leaders. The majority followed the Umayyad dynasty and came to be known as Sunnis. The rest are known as the Shia faction, or the Shiites.

Tribes fought against each other in bloody, ruthless battles.

They fought over land and over religious beliefs. Even though they were all considered Muslim and practiced Islam, the Sunnis felt they were practicing the truth of Islam, and the Shiites felt that their own beliefs corresponded more closely to the truth.

In the mid-18th century, a young scholar named Muhammad bin Abd al-Wahhab became a *Hanbali*. A Hanbali adhered to the strictest of Sunni Muslim laws and opposed more recent and perhaps more liberal practices that had been encroaching on the Islam religion. Some of these practices included loving saints and their tombs, trees, and wells. When people focused their prayers and respect on their saints and on objects rather than on God himself, it was considered idolatry. A Hanbali also saw both extravagance in worship and luxurious living as extreme evils.

Muhammad bin Abd al-Wahhab began teaching his new ideas in his hometown in the Najd (Nejd) area, where foreign traders had not yet brought Western ideas. Most of the people were farmers who struggled to grow crops in this inhospitable land of hot and desolate desert and barren hills, with no access to the sea beyond. It seemed a good place to start preaching his strict Muslim ideas, but even the people here felt that those ideas were too extreme. Just as happened to the Prophet Muhammad, Muhammad bin Abd al-Wahhab's own family drove him out. He took refuge in a nearby town called Diriyah, under the protection of Muhammad bin Saud, the Emir of Diriyah, whose descendents would become the rulers of a greater country two hundred years later. The Emir ruled this small region and was highly respected. Today, an emir is the governor of a city or province.

The people of the Najd area, including the Saud family, grew dates. These fruits were the mainstay of their diet. Many farmers in the area grew dates, and not much else. They were constantly attacked by Bedouin raiders, just as the Prophet

When *Hanbali* al-Wahhab was driven out of his hometown for preaching a stricter form of Islam, he fled here, to the palace of Muhammad bin Saud, Emir of Diriyah. Called the Palace of Sa'd bin Saud, the structure was built in 1446 out of mud bricks.

Muhammad had been attacked by the Bedouins a thousand years earlier.

At this time, in the 18th century, Islam had splintered into many sects. Some areas didn't even believe in Islam. People worshiped objects, rather than any one god. They wore charms to keep evil away and practiced astrology. Muhammad bin Abd al-Wahhab saw this all around him and felt it was his mission to teach and preach true Islam, the way the Prophet Muhammad had done over a thousand years earlier. When Muhammad bin Abd al-Wahhab had lived a year with the Saud family, he and Muhammad bin Saud united to convert people to Islam. This alliance would later be referred to as the Wahhabi Reformation of Islam; it is practiced by the Saudi royal family today.

Together they visited nearby Arab tribes and villages, determined to convert as many people as they could. Not only did they wish to convert people back to the true Islam, they also wished to unite the tribes and people under one god and, eventually, unite the entire Arabian Peninsula. The two men were a strong force. Muhammad bin Abd al-Wahhab was the spiritual leader and spokesperson and Muhammad bin Saud was the military leader and protector of the sect. Their beliefs and ideologies soon became known as the Wahhabi Doctrine, named after Muhammad bin Abd al-Wahhab. The current Al Saud dynasty and the country named Saudi Arabia derive their names from Muhammad bin Saud.

In the late 18th and early 19th centuries, the two men managed to spread their rule and the Wahhabi Doctrine over most of northern Arabia. They even captured the holy city of Mecca and the city of Medina. While there, al-Wahhab and Al Saud destroyed many tombs and shrines that were associated with the Muslim hajj, or pilgrimage. They felt that people were worshiping the actual shrines and not worshiping the one true god.

The Wahhabi Doctrine spread to the Gulf region, into the areas now known as Oman, Kuwait, and Qatar, and even to India, but the sect could not seem to win over the Rashid family and the western part of the Arabian Peninsula. Al Saud, al-Wahhab, and their followers were confined to the central and eastern portions of Arabia.

The Rashid family had the backing of the powerful Ottoman Empire in Turkey. The Ottoman Empire was spreading, working its way into the Arabian Peninsula. It, too, was a Muslim empire, but its people did not believe in the Wahhabi Doctrine. Together, the Rashid family and the Ottoman Empire were a strong force, and it seemed that the Wahhabi Doctrine would not survive.

Battles between tribes and even within the Al Saud household went on for years. In 1875, after much conflict and bloodshed over who would rule the city of Riyadh, the youngest son of King Faisal became king. His name was Abd al-Rahman (or Abdul Rahman) bin Faisal Al Saud. There were constant battles with the Rashid family for control of the city of Riyadh. Finally the Al Saud family was sent into exile; they lost control of the city and any hope they had of unification. Little did they know that Al Saud's and al-Wahhab's vision would succeed, through the efforts of the son of Abdul Rahman bin Faisal.

In 1902, his son, Abd al-Aziz (or Abdul Aziz) bin Abd al-Rahman Al Saud, later known as Ibn Saud, captured the capital city of Riyadh in a bloody battle, and the Rashid family began to crumble. The birth of Saudi Arabia as we know it today began here.

Although he liked the Americans he met, mostly men working for the newly founded Saudi oil company ARAMCO, Abdul Aziz would not allow non-Muslims into the city of Riyadh. If he did invite someone, the guest had to dress in the Arabian style. Today, oil is the major part of the economic ties between the U.S. and Saudi Arabia. Here, an ARAMCO official watches progress at a rig at the al-Howta oil field.

2

Desert Kingdom

Today, many people think of Saudi Arabia as a rich and modern country, and in many ways it is. Because of the country's wealth, it may be regarded as one of the superpowers of the world, as is the United States. The major cities in Saudi Arabia have beautiful, modern buildings complete with air conditioning, a recently added luxury. In other areas of the cities are adobe buildings reminiscent of earlier times.

Until 1945, Saudi Arabia was considered poor and "backward." Called the homeland of Islam, it is where the Prophet Muhammad was born and the great holy city of Mecca is located. Other than that, Saudi Arabia was seen as a desert with very little to offer. In fact, it wasn't even Saudi Arabia until 1932, when the ruler Abdul Aziz bin Saud renamed the country after his family. Before that, it was simply called Arabia.

When Abdul Aziz bin Saud battled against other tribes to unite the country, he did not have the wealth and status of the present-day king. In time, however, things would change. As his vision became reality, wild Arabia would be united under one god and under one ruler.

Today, Saudi Arabia supplies much of the world with oil, or "black gold." This newfound wealth has changed the lives of many Saudis, but most of the power and wealth go to the ruling government, the House of Saud. The Saudi royal family has made many positive changes for its country and the people. However, among the dangers of wealth are corruption and hypocrisy, and the Saudi royal family has been criticized for just these faults.

A NEW TIME

> *"Who will ride at my side on this perilous venture?*
> *Who will risk life and limb to expel Al Rashid?"*
> *Sixty answered my call, young and brave, one and all.*
> *"With all of our strength, we will give what you need;*
> *We will stand by your side when the battle is joined*
> *Until each of us falls—or Riyadh is freed."*

This is a small section taken from a lengthy poem written in honor of King Abdul Aziz, who, after capturing Riyadh in 1902, boldly proclaimed that he was the new emir not just of the small Riyadh region, but of the entire peninsula of Arabia. In the eyes of this new emir and his followers, they succeeded only because God wanted them to succeed.

The Saudis are proud of their history, a history that can still be easily recollected by many elderly citizens. The bloody battle this poem details made a young man a king and founded the kingdom of Saudi Arabia.

Abdul Aziz was born in Riyadh in 1880. When he was ten years old, the Rashid family drove his family out. The family fled to a refuge near Rub' al-Khali (the Empty Quarter) in the

A 1934 photo of Abdul Aziz bin Saud, the first king of Saudi Arabia. The West calls him King bin Saud; Saudi Arabia calls him King Abdul Aziz. The words *bin* and *ibn*, often used interchangeably, mean "son of"; *bint* means "daughter of."

eastern part of the Arabian Peninsula. It is said that young Abdul Aziz and his sister were hidden away in saddlebags carried by a camel. The family lived among a poor tribe called the Bani Murrah. Abdul Aziz learned to ride camels and horses and shoot rifles. He also observed and learned how to deal with other tribal Arabs, something that would prove invaluable later in his life.

The family was eventually given asylum by the sheikh of Kuwait and moved to a fishing port near the head of the Persian Gulf. Here, Abdul Aziz learned about the Ottoman Empire and those who controlled the Arabian Peninsula—the Rashid family. By the 20th century the Ottoman Empire, backed by British rule, was creeping into many Arab countries. The Arabian Peninsula was one of the last places it did not control. Some of the Arab sheikhs made treaties with the British, but young Abdul Aziz bin Saud did not want to be protected by foreign Christians, nor did he want dependency on the Ottomans, whom the Wahhabis saw as untrue Muslims.

Abdul Aziz had bigger ideas and a grander plan for his country. He wanted to retake Riyadh from the Rashid family and realize the dream his great-grandfathers and father had envisioned. He wanted to unite the peninsula of Arabia and make the Wahhabi Doctrine and Sunni Muslim law the chosen doctrine and law of the Islamic religion and Arabia. He wanted to regain the land of his forefathers despite all obstacles. Calling this a *jihad*, or holy war, Abdul Aziz resolved to unify the ranks of his nation under the banner "There is no God but Allah and Muhammad is the Messenger of Allah."

THE TAKING OF RIYADH

It is said that, riding camels, Abdul Aziz and a band of sixty followers raced to his ancestral capital and took it over in 1902. Abdul Aziz was just twenty-two years old. The story itself is frequently told and is perhaps the most dramatic of all modern stories told about Saudi Arabia.

Under cover of night, Abdul Aziz and his cousin, Abdullah bin Jelawi, and several other volunteers stealthily approached a part of the city wall that they knew they could easily scale unobserved. The wall was adjacent to the house of a man who had served Abdul Rahman, Abdul Aziz's father, some years before, when the Saud family had still ruled in Riyadh. The man and his wife helped Abdul Aziz and his men get to the Rashid palace across the city's rooftops.

Abdul Aziz was looking for one member of the Rashid family in particular—Ajlan Rashid, the current emir. Armed with rifles, Abdul Aziz entered Ajlan Rashid's harem. The women and slaves were terrified and quickly told Abdul Aziz the location of Ajlan's bedroom. Abdul Aziz stormed the bedroom of his enemy and found Ajlan's wife and sister. When the wife of this man realized that the son of Abdul Rahman had come to reclaim his birthright, she told Abdul Aziz how many guards were in the palace and described her husband's morning routine.

Some people wonder why this woman so readily betrayed her husband. She was probably more afraid for her own safety than her husband's. Rather than killing the women, Abdul Aziz locked them in a cellar and waited until morning to attack Ajlan and capture the city.

At dawn, after prayers, Ajlan emerged from the mosque into the street. When Ajlan was in the open, Abdul Aziz gave a loud battle cry and rushed from the palace to attack. Ajlan fled with Abdul Aziz and his companions in hot pursuit. Abdul Aziz quickly cornered Ajlan, who defended himself until the sword of Abdullah bin Jelawi killed him.

The unexpected attack and the death of their leader demoralized the Rashid army, whose leaders assumed that such an assault could only have been mounted by a large and well-equipped force. Thinking that the residents of the city had welcomed the return of the Al Saud family, the army surrendered.

When Abdul Aziz took control of Riyadh on January 15, 1902, he burned 1,200 people to death and spiked the heads of other political and tribal enemies as a lesson to the people.

Although Abdul Aziz won that bloody battle, it took him thirty more years to truly unite the Arabian Peninsula. This process involved many more horrific battles, including Bedouin raids and wars between the Saudi-Wahhabi and other contenders for power.

At the turn of the 20th century, Arabia had so many rulers that they could not all be documented. Abdul Aziz and his loyal followers had to defeat these tribal leaders one by one. First they defeated the Ottoman-backed Rashid family. In 1906, they gradually won control over the tribes of central and eastern Arabia. Abdul Aziz conquered the kingdom of Hijaz (or Hejaz) and took control of the holy cities of Mecca and Medina between 1924 and 1926.

Soon, Abdul Aziz became the most respected leader in Arabia, though some of this may have been more fear than true respect. Abdul Aziz personally executed eighteen rebellious tribal chiefs. He chose his provincial governors for their brutality, not their compassion. To tighten their grip on the kingdom, these governors executed 40,000 people and amputated the limbs of another 350,000 out of a population of four million.

KEEPING CONTROL

With so many warring tribes, it seems hard to fathom how one man and a small group of supporters took over a country and retained their power. Now that he was the king of Arabia and leader of the Wahhabi sect, Abdul Aziz first saw to it that Wahhabi Islam was strictly enforced and followed. His many followers were Bedouin—people who seemed to enjoy fighting and winning. Abdul Aziz used religious beliefs to reinforce their desire to protect their new king and all he stood for.

Many saw Abdul Aziz as brave and strong, having conquered so much in a short time. His courageous exploits and personal magnetism drew people to him; thousands of

"There is no God but Allah, and Muhammad is the Messenger of Allah." Under this banner, Abdul Aziz's soldiers took the capital city of Riyadh in 1902 and then went on to conquer the kingdoms of Hijaz and Asir. In this 1928 photograph, his soldiers march through the mountains toward Iraq and Transjordan.

Arabs loved and obeyed him. If he had won so victoriously, Allah himself must have blessed him.

> On that night long ago, when the time came to act,
> I knew in my heart what it was to be free;
> The greatest good fortune in life for a man is
> To know he has reached for the best he can be.
> Whatever might follow that cold, moonless night
> We would know we had fought for a cause that was right.
>
> —excerpt from the poem celebrating
> Abdul Aziz's taking of Riyadh

Abdul Aziz was skilled not just in the martial arts such as

hand-to-hand combat, but also in the "marital arts." He married and divorced so many women, it's hard to keep track of all of them. To Westerners this seems like a most peculiar practice, but during Abdul Aziz's day, marriage was used to seal peace and retain unity among the tribes he had defeated. However, Koranic law states that a man may have only four wives at once, so after making peace Abdul Aziz divorced his new wife and returned her to her home with gifts.

Abdul Aziz had nearly three hundred wives during his lifetime. Many of these women he married only for a day. He probably never saw their faces, as women were required to remain veiled even on their wedding night. However, it was said that every woman who married Abdul Aziz fell madly in love with him and loved him for the rest of her life. Of course, this is part of the legend of Abdul Aziz bin Saud and how he conquered Arabia!

Always thinking of ways to unite the tribes under one king, Abdul Aziz created a religious organization called *Ikhwan*, which meant "brotherhood." Members of the Ikhwan were persuaded to give up their Bedouin way of life, which meant giving up camel nomadism and settling in one place. By doing so, they were obeying the Wahhabi teachings. They never actually became farmers, but they did settle in small agricultural villages where Abdul Aziz had more control over them and could call upon them to serve him. Without the Ikhwan, the Saudis probably couldn't have united Arabia in such a short time. However, the Ikhwan would eventually become unruly and bloodthirsty and turn on Abdul Aziz.

After capturing Asir, the kingdom between Hijaz and Yemen, Abdul Aziz was unable to conquer the rest of the Arabian Peninsula. On September 22, 1932, he declared that Arabia was now Saudi Arabia and that Abdul Aziz was its only king. He attempted to capture Yemen in a brief war a couple of years later, but this proved futile. Abdul Aziz knew his limits; he seemed satisfied that the dream of his forefathers had now become reality.

King Abdul Aziz bin Saud was not a rich man, even though he was king. The new Saudi Arabia was still a very poor country. Abdul Aziz united the country through his devotion to Islam but his puritanical beliefs could not withstand the wealth and westernization that his beloved country would soon face.

King Abdul Aziz in 1943. He was the sole ruler, governor, lawmaker, and social worker to his new country, and led it through both World War I and World War II. Until the postwar industrial boom that began in 1947, the kingdom was on the verge of financial ruin.

3

King Abdul Aziz—A New Kingdom

Just as the sands in a desert shift and change, so did the leadership of the Arabian Peninsula. What was once wild territory governed by numerous nomadic tribes suddenly became a united country with one name, one king, and one government. Saudi Arabia was born; the country and its king, Abdul Aziz bin Saud, governed by strict Islamic law.

In 1912, King Abdul Aziz attempted to organize young men from the different tribes into an army to work for the common good of not just the people but also the new country. This was a daunting task because it required bringing together people who had been fighting each other for years. The new army consisted mostly of Bedouin tribesmen who only knew and understood desert combat; Abdul Aziz found it difficult to keep them under control. They killed, plundered, and raped, all in the name of Allah. In just a few years, they became so fanatical that even their own Bedouin Code of Law meant nothing to them. Sadly, Abdul Aziz saw his army, his warriors for Allah, become the very thing he and those of the Wahhabi sect despised—relentless renegades.

Abdul Aziz had other problems, as well. He'd killed Ajlan Rashid, but the Rashid family remained. The Rashid family had its own army in the north. Battles between the two families continued for ten more years.

In the meantime, war on a much larger scale was being waged: World War I. The European armies cared little about the desert land of Arabia, but the British did want to enlist the cooperation of the new Arab leader in their fight against the Ottomans, who were still supporting the Rashid family. Two British men, Sir Percy Cox and William Shakespeare (not to be confused with the writer, William Shakespeare) befriended Abdul Aziz. The British often encouraged Abdul Aziz to attack the Rashid family's ancestral home in Hail.

The British supported Abdul Aziz in the war against the Ottoman Empire and the Rashid family, but they supported another man as ruler of the unified Arabian Peninsula. The British favored Husayn, the Hashemite sharif of Mecca, not Abdul Aziz. Obviously this did not please Abdul Aziz, who refrained from attacking Husayn only because the British opposed it, and Abdul Aziz had an alliance with the British.

Thomas Edward Lawrence was an archaeologist for the British Museum Archaeological Expedition in Mesopotamia who stayed in the Middle East after the outbreak of World War I and learned Arabic. He also wished to see a united Arabia. In 1916, he joined Faisal I, who was the son of Husayn, the sharif of Mecca, in the fight against the Ottoman Empire. He became known as Lawrence of Arabia. His book, entitled *The Seven Pillars of Wisdom: A Triumph*, described his Arabian adventures.

Meanwhile, the Ikhwan were gaining more strength and power. They promoted their religious beliefs of Wahhabism

Faisal I, son of Sherif Husayn of Mecca, stands in front of his party in this 1918 photograph taken at a post–World War I peace conference in Paris. One of the delegates in his party was T.E. Lawrence (third from the right), who gained fame as Lawrence of Arabia. The British favored Husayn for rule of the Arabian Peninsula, rather than Abdul Aziz.

and calmed the occasional rebellion, but they disobeyed Abdul Aziz's commands and broke the very laws of the religion they were trying to spread.

In 1919, the British turned their backs on Abdul Aziz and threw their support behind Sherif Husayn of Mecca, naming him the ruler of Arabia. The sharif of Mecca had already declared himself king of Arabia in 1917.

When a dispute arose over control of land between Hijaz and Najd in 1919, the sharif organized thousands of men and marched to the area. They easily overran a town called Turabah and thought they were victorious. Little did they know that the ruthlessness of the Ikhwan, under the leadership of Abdul Aziz, would change all this, and quickly. On the night of March 25, 1919, the Ikhwan attacked without warning. They recaptured Turabah and in the process killed 6,000 men. It is said that Abdul Aziz cried openly at the sight. Abdul Aziz ordered the Ikhwan not to pursue Husayn's fleeing army to the town of Taif. Surprisingly, they obeyed.

In 1920, Abdul Aziz turned his attention to the Rashid family. In this, Abdul Aziz once again demonstrated his strong character and his faithfulness to his religion.

An eighteen-year-old boy was the ruler of the Rashid family. He became the head of the household only after a number of murders occurred, including the murders of his father and cousin. He was weak, both physically and in spirit, and just as afraid of his own family as he was of Abdul Aziz. Knowing how other family members felt about him, the young Rashid decided that his chances were better with Abdul Aziz than with his own family. As Abdul Aziz's army approached, he fled the city of Hail dressed as a woman and begged Abdul Aziz for mercy.

Would Abdul Aziz show compassion or would he have the young boy beheaded? After all, this boy represented Abdul Aziz's archenemy, the Rashid family. Abdul Aziz showed great mercy and restraint. He did storm the palace of Rashid, and a battle raged for several days. The Rashid family finally surrendered. Abdul Aziz could easily have had them all killed. Instead, he told them that if they surrendered, they would be pardoned.

In front of the Rashid family, witnessed by the Ikhwan and many others, Abdul Aziz said something amazing: "I wish to assure you that you are as my sons and that you will live in Riyadh just as I and my sons live, no more, no less. Your clothes, food and horses will be like mine, if not better. There will be nothing in my palace or in the country that, if you want it, you cannot have. If any one of you has any doubt about what I say, let him speak"

No one said a word. After a few more words of promise, Abdul Aziz extended his hand to the Rashid family. He won his enemies over with his kindness. Sticking to his promises, Abdul Aziz fed the people of Hail and took the widow of the former Rashid ruler as his own wife. He also adopted all of the widows and children, a thousand in all! The intense rivalry between the House of Rashid and the House of Saud was over.

Now Abdul Aziz had to deal with his own creation, the Ikhwan. No longer obeying Abdul Aziz, they attacked villages, cities, and innocent people all over northern Arabia. Many people were so terrified of the Ikhwan that the people of a town would pack and leave if they heard of the Ikhwan's approach. Success after success only encouraged their belief that they were God's warriors, eliminating all that was evil in the eyes of God.

Spoiling for a fight, Ikhwan raiders attacked a Wahhabi caravan—their own people. They killed the men, boys, and male babies and left the women wandering hopelessly around the corpses. Abdul Aziz had heard and seen enough. He brought together an army of loyal Bedouins and met the Ikhwan at the oasis of Sibilla on March 29, 1929. The battle itself was brief; the Ikhwan were outnumbered.

Although clearly defeated, the Ikhwan army did not go away. They reorganized and grew in number over the next year. But so did Abdul Aziz's army. Determined to put an end to the Ikhwan, Abdul Aziz mechanized his army. An Englishman named Philby, the import agent for Ford motorcars in Arabia, encouraged Abdul Aziz to use cars instead of camels. The sight of fast-moving metal machines in battle totally demoralized the Ikhwan. The old ways of Arabia were giving way to those of the West, to more modern times. How could a camel compete with a car? It couldn't and neither could the Ikhwan.

The Ikhwan leader, al-Duwaish, and his family sought refuge in Kuwait, where he surrendered with the condition that the British would take responsibility for all his women and children. The British agreed, and a man named Dickson took in al-Duwaish's family. Dickson then pleaded with Abdul Aziz to spare al-Duwaish's life. Abdul Aziz said he would spare al-Duwaish's life if all of the Ikhwan leaders were handed over to him.

When Dickson asked about al-Duwaish's family, Abdul Aziz responded, "His daughters will be my daughters, his sisters, my sisters." Again, Abdul Aziz took in the family of his enemy, demonstrating to his country his compassion and devotion to Islam.

UNITED SAUDI ARABIA

Although Abdul Aziz united the peninsula of Arabia, the last twenty years of his life would prove to be his loneliest and most desolate. The 1930s were particularly hard for the new king. The country had no money and the only income came from the taxes that pilgrims paid when traveling to Mecca from all over the peninsula for the yearly hajj. This was not enough to sustain a kingdom and its people. Some money also came in from oil, but the development of oil had only just begun.

The greatest need was food, in this country that could barely grow food. Saudi Arabia had to import food from other countries. Because Saudi Arabia had little money, the purchase of food left the country in debt to other countries. The situation seemed hopeless. Modern times and realities were plaguing Abdul Aziz and he became more depressed.

Abdul Aziz was a great ruler, but he had no administrative experience. Now that Abdul Aziz had his united country under Islam and one God, he did not really know how to operate it. His instinct told him to rule as he did in the desert. If a person

From 1947 on, the Saudi royal family could indeed live like princes. Suddenly Abdul Aziz's sons found the rest of the world just an airplane ride away. In 1947, four of his sons and one grandson accompanied him to New York as part of a delegation to the United Nations. Prince Faisal (center), who would become king of Saudi Arabia in 1964, was Saudi Arabia's permanent delegate to the United Nations.

asked him for money to help buy food or medicine, Abdul Aziz gave it to him. It never occurred to the great king to set up some kind of ministry to take care of the medical, social, and economic needs of many people.

The kingdom itself was isolated. The capital of Riyadh, in the middle of the peninsula, enticed few Westerners—in fact, non-Muslims were not allowed into the city. Abdul Aziz himself had been out of the country just once, to visit Iraq.

In 1936 and 1939, Abdul Aziz granted oil concessions to American companies, allowing them to explore and drill for oil. The oil deposits of Arabia proved to be among the richest in the world, and Abdul Aziz used some of the income derived from them on national improvements. The greater part of his oil revenues, however, went to the royal family.

In 1939, World War II created more problems for the king. Being a Muslim, he did not care for Jews and could have sided with the German Nazis, as they would have liked. He decided the best stand for Saudi Arabia would be to stay neutral. Cutbacks in oil production ensued because of the war and America's focus on the war effort. As well, fewer people made the pilgrimage to Mecca. The income from taxes subsided and the kingdom was near financial ruin.

When World War II ended, the United States showed a renewed interest in Saudi oil. With the help of the United States, oil production boomed and a cordial relationship developed between Abdul Aziz and President Roosevelt.

At this time, there was great concern for the Jewish and Palestinian people. World War II had displaced millions of Jewish people, and the battle over Israel grew between Jews and Arabs. Abdul Aziz told Roosevelt he sympathized with the Jews, but he felt they should have their Jewish state in Germany, not Palestine. Roosevelt asked Abdul Aziz to meet with the Jewish leader, Chaim Weizman, but Abdul Aziz refused, saying he was not the spokesperson for the Arab world.

Oil production increased dramatically during the postwar industrial boom. From 1947 on, Saudi Arabia never had to worry about debt, bankruptcy, or reliance on other countries— at least, this is what was thought. History has proven otherwise. Regardless, the money made from oil was more than anything ever dreamed of by the king or his family. Rather than making Abdul Aziz happy, though, this new wealth and his own children broke his heart and made him a lonely, bitter man in the last years of his life.

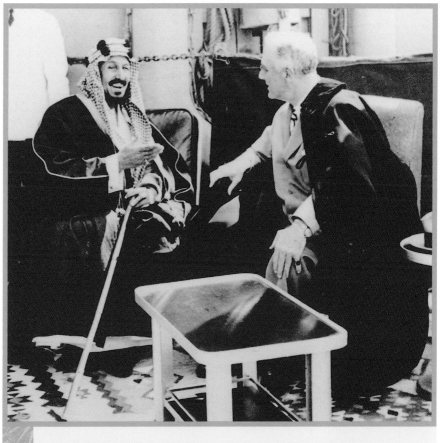

King Abdul Aziz met with U.S. President Roosevelt aboard a U.S. warship near Cairo, Egypt in 1945. A cordial relationship developed between the two leaders.

Each family member was given an allowance in the thousands of dollars, and soon the West became that much closer—just an airplane ride away. The young Saudi princes, who had led relatively sheltered lives in the desert until this time, discovered grand cities such as London, Paris, and New York. With money came luxuries: homes, cars, Western clothing, and women. With money, the ideals of Islam that Abdul Aziz treasured seemed to be forgotten.

When Prince Mousaad was caught dancing naked in a

"Nubaik ala Kitab Allah wa Sinnat a rasoul Allah."–"We pledge loyalty to you on the Book of God and the traditions of his Messenger." The sons and grandsons of King Abdul Aziz spoke these words to Saud IV just minutes after the king's death made Saud the new king of Saudi Arabia. King Saud is shown here with his father, King Abdul Aziz (seated).

fountain in Paris he was immediately sent home, and Abdul Aziz confined his son to the palace. Mousaad became angry with his father. Although unable to act upon his anger, it showed years later.

Another son, Prince Mishari, killed the British consul in Jeddah because the consul refused to give him some whiskey. As is dictated by Islam law, Abdul Aziz offered the family of the consul his own son's life. They refused, but Abdul Aziz felt his son should be punished and put him in prison. Mishari's brother, Saud, who became king after the death of Abdul Aziz, later pardoned the prince.

In early November of 1953, news spread that King Abdul Aziz of Saudi Arabia was dying. His sons and grandsons left their homes all over the world and rushed to the king's bedside. On November 9, Abdul Aziz bin Saud died surrounded by forty sons and sixty grandsons. Just minutes after Abdul Aziz died, his eldest living son, Saud IV, was declared the new king.

The body of King Abdul Aziz was buried in the desert sand at Miqbarat al-Oud. Only two rocks marked his grave, one at his head and the other at his feet, because Wahhabi tradition stipulates that there be no inscription on the grave. He was buried next to his favorite sister, Nura—the sister he had shared a saddlebag with sixty years earlier, when they were exiled to Kuwait. He left behind him a dynasty of many princes and princesses, 6,000 family members, and a country filled with black gold.

Today there are no graves. The rocks have been covered by sand, and the king has returned to his desert once again.

King Saud founded Riyadh University in 1957, the year in which this photo was taken. Riyadh University was renamed King Saud University in 1982. The university has allowed women to enroll as students since the early 1960s.

4

King Saud, the Black Sheikh: 1953–1964

When King Abdul Aziz died, his son Saud inherited the kingdom. Scholars are not certain why Abdul Aziz chose Saud. Born in 1902, he was the second son, always living in the shadow of his older brother, Turki. Saud's mother, Wadha bint Hazami, was a member of the Bani Khalid tribe.

Abdul Aziz provided for the educated of all his sons. At the time, this was called a "court education," which simply meant that they were taught to read in Arabic. Part of this education included memorizing the Koran, which Saud did before his 14th birthday. Boys learned to read, write, and do arithmetic, but they also took lessons in desert warfare.

Turki was clearly Abdul Aziz's favorite son, not just because he was the oldest boy, but because he had become an expert horseman and a courageous warrior by the time he was 12 years old. Saud was often ill, and although he grew tall like his father, he was weak and had poor eyesight. Had Turki lived, there is little doubt that he would have been named king of Saudi Arabia after his father's death.

Just after World War I, the Spanish flu swept through parts of the Arabian Peninsula. The Al Saud family was hit hard. The flu took the lives of two younger sons and eventually one of Abdul Aziz's wives, the mother of Khalid, another son destined to be king. And it took the life of Turki. Abdul Aziz turned to Saud to take over the role of his older brother. Saud was not the horseman his brother had been, though he did join his father in battle against the House of Rashid and proved to be a brave fighter. In 1926, he rode again into battle with his father against the sharif of Mecca. During this battle, some say, four assassins surrounded Abdul Aziz and Saud and knocked Abdul Aziz unconscious. Saud protected his father and defended himself against the assassins, killing one and holding off the others until help arrived. Saud proved himself loyal to his father and family, but his reputation would change drastically over time.

Again, however, the older brother faced competition with the younger: Saud and Faisal. The term "sibling rivalry" can be applied to its fullest extent when it comes to the Saudi royal family. Islamic law states that a man can have as many as four wives. The sons all have the same father, but they don't have the same mother, which makes them half-brothers. Perhaps sibling loyalty was not as strong as it might have been had the sons of Abdul Aziz been born of the same mother.

As king, Abdul Aziz had to assess each son's ability and utilize that son's strengths. Feelings were no doubt hurt when one son was chosen over another, which is exactly what happened between Saud and Faisal. Abdul Aziz chose Faisal to lead an attack on Jeddah. There was a foreign diplomatic community in Jeddah and Abdul Aziz felt Faisal could best

Saud and his half-brother Faisal were rivals for their father's attention. While King Abdul Aziz kept Saud in Riyadh as viceroy of Najd, Faisal traveled to Europe and the U.S., gaining experience in foreign affairs and diplomacy. In 1946, Faisal and his son, Muhammad bin Faisal bin Abd al-Aziz Al Saud, attended a Palestine conference in London, England.

handle this particular situation because of his experience with foreign governments. Saud felt slighted by his father and wrote to him of his anger. It was obvious to Abdul Aziz that he would have to divide the responsibilities up. He gave Faisal and his third eldest son, Muhammad, responsibility for the Ikhwan. He kept Saud in Riyadh and made him viceroy of the Najd. Although governing the area as viceroy was an important responsibility, Saud felt that his father did not favor him.

Saud's duties included upholding the Wahhabi code of behavior. Saud tried to emulate his father in his compassion towards the people and in handling disputes between tribes, but he lacked two important qualities: charm and intelligence. He may have been book-smart, but Saud lacked skill in the fine art of foreign policy and diplomacy, something in which Faisal was gaining experience. Perhaps Saud's lack of knowledge had more to do with the fact that Abdul Aziz himself never ventured from the Arabian Peninsula. His only contact with foreign diplomats came when they traveled to him. Much of what Saud knew, he learned by watching his father. Faisal, on the other hand, traveled to Europe and the United States. He understood Western ways and became fluent in English. These would become important things for a future king of modern-day Saudi Arabia to know.

Because of Saud's lack of knowledge in foreign diplomacy, he felt he was treated in a belittling way by some of the greatest leaders in the world. One of his first visits with Harry S. Truman, the President of the United States in 1947, proved to be a fiasco—at least, in the eyes of Saud. Although Saud wanted to discuss important issues concerning Palestine and other matters, Truman seemed more interested in what Saud was wearing, his mannerisms, and his entourage.

Much of the West had stereotyped the Arab population as being more interested in trinkets and bobbles than foreign policy. Truman presented Saud with a World War II medal for meritorious service to the Allied cause. This was ridiculous, since Saudi Arabia had entered the war just two months before it ended, and not one Saudi saw combat. One good thing came from Saud's visit to the United States: the first U.S. embassy was established in Riyadh in 1949.

When Saud IV became king of Saudi Arabia, the 40 sons and 60 grandsons who were present at the deathbed of Abdul Aziz welcomed Saud to his new position and swore loyalty to him. Faisal even kissed him on the shoulders and the bridge of his nose, a sign of both affection and respect. Faisal was just as loyal to the new king as anyone else. King Saud kept Faisal as the viceroy of the Hijaz and as foreign minister.

As King Saud assumed his new role, it was obvious to some that he could not be the kind of king this new country needed in order to survive. The Middle East was undergoing harsh changes in the early 1950s. The Arab nations wanted to get away from British and French imperialism, seeing the presence of Great Britain and France in the region as the source of many injustices. Some Arab nations felt they had been exploited solely for the benefit of these Western countries.

What really angered the Arab world was the creation of Israel. Many Middle Eastern countries felt Arab land was stolen from them for its creation. To people like King Abdul Aziz and King Saud, this represented a great betrayal by a country they had once trusted—Great Britain. This betrayal led those in the Arab countries to rethink what had happened to them in the past.

The biggest issue was oil. As Iran concluded that its resources were being stolen by Great Britain and the United States, others began questioning their alliance with these two countries, as well. The British government was keeping the price of oil low, which created an industrial and economic boom in the West, particularly in western Europe, but also kept the nations of the Middle East in underdevelopment and poverty. King Saud, like his father, decided to support and promote Arab and Islamic unity.

In the early 1950s, at the height of the Cold War, extremists rallied in the Middle East and disputes arose between Arab nations such as Egypt and Saudi Arabia. There was also the threat of invasion by the Soviet Union to the north. One thing Saudi Arabia had in its favor was that the United States opposed the Soviet Union as much as they did.

About this time, Saud found himself in financial trouble.

Saudi oil refineries at Ras Tanura on the Persian Gulf in 1956.

He had been spending so much money building palaces and mansions that he nearly ran his country into debt. He turned to ARAMCO (the Arabian American Oil Company) for help. In turn, ARAMCO passed through Congress a "tax credit" bill. This bill provided King Saud with a massive subsidy, money that normally the U.S. Treasury would have received. Unbeknownst to them, the American taxpayers made up for the losses through taxation.

It was rumored that, when Saud finished building a $50 million palace, he joked that he should send a thank-you card to the American people. Dwight D. Eisenhower, then-president of the United States, remained quiet over this injustice to the American people. He saw King Saud as a way "in," a way to gain the loyalty of other Arab nations through his own invention, the Eisenhower Doctrine.

The Eisenhower Doctrine was developed to suppress Soviet expansion. It provided military assistance to countries threatened by communism. President Eisenhower, who became president of the United States in 1953, needed an Arab spokesperson and Saud would be that spokesperson. The two men met and debated over the benefits to Saudi Arabia if Saud supported this doctrine. In the end, Saud walked away with American tanks, aircraft, arms, ammunition, and the services of military personnel in training the Saudi armed forces, as well as a loan for $250 million. Eisenhower agreed to put pressure on Israel to withdraw from Gaza if Saud would be the spokesperson for the doctrine.

On his return to Saudi Arabia, King Saud made stops in Morocco, Tunisia, Libya, and Egypt. In Egypt he met with hostility; Egypt's President Nasser disagreed with much of what Saud had to say. The Eisenhower Doctrine created further dissension between the two countries, who were already in dispute.

(Years later, many believe, King Saud arranged for the assassination of President Nasser. Saud's reputation was already sinking, and this attempt on the life of Nasser did not improve the situation. The evidence against Saud was indisputable. Although King Saud said he would launch an investigation, it never happened, some would say because he knew he would be

Seen here with U.S. President Eisenhower (left) and Vice President Nixon in Washington, D.C. in 1957, King Saud agreed to support the Eisenhower Doctrine in return for U.S. military equipment and a loan of $250 million.

found guilty of an attempt on President Nasser's life and be disgraced. As the sole ruler of Saudi Arabia, he was able to prevent any investigation into this plot.)

What had Saud done for his people? There were no plans for the future development of Saudi Arabia, no reforms. His spending escalated; he spent $150 million to build the Forbidden City, a private city that included four separate palaces, one for each wife. It also included 32 mansions for his concubines, 37 villas to house his sons, schools, a hospital, a museum, a zoo, and the largest air conditioning plant in the world. Inside, the palaces were decorated with reproduction Louis XIV furniture, tables inlaid with gold and silver, crystal chandeliers and fixtures, and Persian carpets. This complex was just one of about 50 of Saud's projects.

His flamboyant spending did not go unnoticed. Many Saudis disliked Saud and the royal family. After all, many of the members of the royal family who claimed to be devout Wahhabi Muslims were breaking the basic laws taught by Islam. Saud was also overly generous to others with his wealth. He had been seen tipping hotel workers the equivalent of hundreds of American dollars. Unfortunately for the royal family, his bad reputation didn't remain with him but spread to the rest of the Saud household. The royal family gained a reputation for extravagance.

Meanwhile, his younger brother Faisal observed all these occurrences. In 1958, the senior Al Saud princes realized they would face devastating consequences if they did not do something about King Saud. They approached Saud and asked him for his abdication, or resignation, from the throne. Although Faisal saw Saud's behavior as destructive to the royal family, he didn't necessarily want Saud to step down. Instead he wanted his brother to stay on as king, but be more of a figurehead than a true ruler. All power and control of the kingdom would be handed over to Faisal. And Faisal would ensure that his brother remained in his control, as well.

King Saud agreed, but the agreement did not last long. King Saud did not like being just the figurehead of the royal family. He worked to gain support among his few loyal followers.

In the meantime, Faisal was busy strengthening the Saudi economy and repairing the damage his brother had done. He borrowed half a billion riyals (Saudi currency) from a wealthy Saudi banker and assigned the financial genius Anwar Ali to head SAMA, the Saudi Arabian Monetary Agency. His efforts eventually brought the kingdom out of debt.

Faisal's other important objective was to unite the Arab world. He declared that Saudi Arabia would maintain a neutral stance in international affairs, including those regarding

Israel. This latter resolution would be more difficult to uphold than fixing the kingdom's economy had been.

By 1960, Faisal's health was beginning to deteriorate. When he traveled to Switzerland for treatment, King Saud stepped in and took over until Faisal's return. When Saud became ill in 1961 and left for treatment in Europe and the United States, Faisal took over the duties and responsibilities of head of state. During Saud's absence, Faisal replaced Saud's sons, who had positions in the government, with senior princes loyal to Faisal.

No one seemed to know who was really in charge, and there was much confusion in Riyadh. The friction between the two rulers divided both the royal family and the government into two camps: those loyal to Faisal and those loyal to Saud. The division was apparent to other countries in the Middle East, who saw it as a sign that the royal family was on the verge of disintegrating and the kingdom was ripe for a revolution.

To the south of Saudi Arabia lies the country of Yemen. One of those supporting the country in its war to remain independent from Saudi Arabia was the former Egyptian president, Nasser. Nasser was now the president of the union of Egypt and Syria known as the United Arab Republic. Nasser was also backed by the Soviet Union. While Faisal was again out of the country, Egyptian jets bombed towns just over the Saudi border, and Saud was unable to cope.

At the royal family's urging, Faisal quickly returned and the situation began to change. The first reform Saudi Arabia ever saw was put into place. It was called the Ten Points of Policy and was enacted on November 6, 1962.

By the end of November, Faisal had broken all diplomatic relations with Egypt. The air raids increased; by 1963, Yemen was said to have 30,000 Egyptian troops at its disposal.

King Saud and his supporters were still vying for a place in the government and it was still unclear who was the true

Well-wishers surround Faisal after his proclamation as king of Saudi Arabia on November 3, 1964. Faisal had served as prime minister while Saud was king.

king. Faisal stood his ground. He made stronger decisions, especially in the fight against Yemen. Saud realized that he was losing any support he might have in the royal family. Saud's sons instigated conspiracies to overthrow Faisal. One attempted coup was thwarted.

Faisal, feeling tremendous pressure from his family and his country, left Riyadh on a journey overland, seeking solitude away from the confusion. During this time, more than 100 Al Saud princes met and discussed what should happen to their family and the government. They decided that Saud should completely abdicate his throne and Faisal should be the sole ruler. It seemed to them that Faisal had everyone's best interests at heart and was clearly working to make changes that would protect and benefit Saudi Arabia and the way of life of its citizens.

Saud neither agreed to this nor abdicated the throne. Regardless, the Al Saud family recognized Faisal as the new king and placed Saud under house arrest. Still defiant, Saud tried to gather supporters. He failed and, with his wives and a number of sons, Saud was exiled to Athens, Greece. He died there in 1969.

Until recently, the royal family of Saudi Arabia never acknowledged Saud's role as king. His reputation in his later years for incompetence and extravagance overshadowed all the good he'd done in his earlier years. At one time, his portrait was not displayed anywhere in Saudi Arabia. All references to him or his reign were removed from books. The Saudis seemed to be embarrassed to talk about him and referred to him as "the black sheikh of the family."

Perhaps King Saud had trouble in handling the conflict created by living life as a devout Muslim on the one hand and having the riches of the world on the other. While he had the four wives allowed by Islamic doctrine, he also had up to 100 concubines, or mistresses. He spent most of the kingdom's money, about $200 million a year. Yet others have described him as being deeply religious, a good father to his people, and a staunch opponent of communism. These opposing aspects of his personality and behavior show just how complex a man King Saud really was, and they suggest the difficulty of ruling a country that is undergoing rapid and extensive changes.

Today King Saud is recognized among the kings of Saudi Arabia. His picture is now hung in public places. His name is no longer deleted from books, and buildings are being named after him.

King Saud's achievements include: protecting the country's independence and safeguarding its identity; establishing ministries in education, agriculture, commerce, and industry; paving the roads; developing the army; and founding Koran memorization schools.

King Faisal actively promoted economic and educational programs. He was assassinated in 1975.

5

King Faisal, the Hero: 1964–1975

I pray God to give me strength and make me worthy of the trust you put in me. . . . I am one of you, both a brother and a servant. . . . In serving you, I pledge you my loyalty—I will be just to great and small alike.
KING FAISAL

If Saud was known as the disgrace of the family, Faisal was considered its hero. He was born in 1906. Abdul Aziz sent him to Europe just after World War I, which gave him a wider worldview than his brother Saud. What Saud didn't do for his country, Faisal did. He improved its economic, industrial, and agricultural condition by launching agricultural projects that included the Irrigation and Drainage Project and the Sands Project in Al Ahsa, in the kingdom's Eastern region. This was combined with the Haradh Agricultural Project, the Abha Dam Project in the south, the

Aforestation Project, the Animal Resources Project, and the Agricultural Credit Bank to improve conditions in the country. During King Faisal's reign, the area used for agricultural purposes increased greatly and the search for water sources was encouraged. The General Corporation for Petroleum and Minerals was established to help search for mineral deposits throughout the kingdom.

Faisal also improved conditions for women and increased their resources and higher education. Until this time, girls were not educated. Now girls were able to attend schools and young women had more opportunities to attend colleges and universities. He allowed the State to give financial aid and free textbooks to those who needed them. This did not go over well with some people, mainly extremist Wahhabis who believed girls should not be educated. Riots broke out preventing young girls from attending school. However, these riots were minor compared to the riots that occurred at the introduction of the television.

The Koran forbids any representation of the human form. The portrayal of the human form on every television channel broke this law, or so many thought. Faisal argued that the television could be used not for evil, but for good; it could help spread Islam. In 1966, a riot broke out and young Prince Mousaad, the very same prince who was earlier caught dancing naked in a fountain in Paris, was shot and killed by a police-man. Mousaad's father wanted the police officer killed, but after examining all the evidence, Faisal refused. He said the policeman was doing his job and that Mousaad was part of the riot. The father of Mousaad said his son was simply standing by, perhaps in the wrong place at the wrong time. Faisal stood his ground on the issue. The anger and bitterness created by this decision would ultimately cost King Faisal his life.

Much of Faisal's success is credited to one of his wives, Iffat, who was the niece of one of Faisal's friends who had recently died. Faisal helped his friend's widow financially and soon the widow arrived in Riyadh, at Faisal's doorstep, with Iffat and her half-brother, Kamal Adham. Faisal married Iffat just weeks later in an arranged marriage, as all marriages were arranged, and still are in many instances today.

Although it doesn't often happen, Faisal fell in love with his new bride. Many of his marriages to other women ended in divorce, but Faisal and Iffat were married for forty years. Iffat was different from other Arab women because she was educated and westernized. She encouraged her husband to send their sons to the United States for their education. The daughters were also educated, even though there were no schools for girls in Saudi Arabia at the time. They memorized the Koran, learned to read and write in three different languages, and traveled throughout Europe. An old adage says "behind every great man is a great woman" and many attribute Faisal's success to the influence of his intelligent wife. It was her influence that convinced Faisal to open schools for girls and allow the first women's organization, Al Nahda Women's Club.

Iffat's half-brother, Kamal Adham, was close to Faisal and one of the few men Faisal trusted. Kamal Adham advised Faisal on various policies and developed an impressive espionage system, one of the best in the world.

Faisal clearly was not happy with the United States. He did not like the Soviet Union, either. Faisal felt that both countries were invading Arab land. The United States supported the Jews in Israel rather than Palestine—land he saw as Arab land that should be occupied by Arabs. The Soviet backing of Yemen and Nasser was a continual threat.

In 1967, Nasser and Faisal had a common enemy: Israel. During the Six-Day War, Israel occupied the Golan Heights, the Sinai, and Jerusalem. Of course, relations with the United States only got worse when President Nixon told Faisal that he would pressure the Israeli government to withdraw from the territories they recently obtained if Faisal would convince Anwar Sadat, the president of Egypt, to reduce the Soviet military

Israeli troops enter Gaza City in the Gaza Strip in June of 1967. Faisal, like many Arabs, did not understand why the U.S. supported the Jews in their efforts to occupy what he considered Arab land.

presence in Egypt. Faisal kept his word but Nixon did not. Israel refused to negotiate. This betrayal by America prompted Faisal to encourage an oil embargo against the United States.

Hoping to develop stronger ties with other Arab nations such as Kuwait, Jordan, Bahrain, and the United Arab Emirates, he scheduled a meeting with a group of Kuwaiti delegates on March 25, 1975, to discuss matters of unity and the oil embargo. A stranger entered as the men filed into the room. He was the brother of Mousaad, the young prince who had been killed by the policeman and whose death King Faisal wouldn't avenge.

The King recognized the prince and bent his head down so the prince could kiss the bridge of his nose. Instead, the prince pulled a gun from his *thobe* (the long shirt worn by Arab men) and shot the king three times in the face.

Saudi men visit King Faisal's grave on the outskirts of Riyadh a few days after his assassination, in late March of 1975. Wahhabi tradition prohibits any inscription on the grave.

A quick trial found the brother of Mousaad guilty of murder and he was sentenced to death. He was beheaded with a golden sword, as was the right of Saudi princes.

Faisal's reign came to an abrupt and sad end. Along with members of the Al Saud family, heads of state attended his funeral, including Vice President Nelson Rockefeller from the United States. Many Saudis revered Faisal. He brought the country out of the past and into the present—a change that would continue into the reign of the next king, Khalid.

King Faisal accomplished many things during his rule, including increasing the amount of land for agriculture and expanding the search for sources of water, expanding higher education and providing more educational opportunities for girls, and safeguarding the country's independence and its identity.

Khalid (shown here in 1974) became king in 1975. Because of his calm demeanor, many thought Khalid would not be a good ruler. He proved them wrong. He continued his brother Faisal's legacy by promoting Arab unity and making Saudi Arabia a more modern country, independent from others.

6

King Khalid, the Quiet One: 1975–1982

Each of the rulers of Saudi Arabia had their own personality and way of doing things. King Khalid was no different. Born in Riyadh in 1913, Khalid bin Abd al-Aziz was brought up under the watchful eye of his father, King Abdul Aziz Al Saud. This religious upbringing shaped his morals and his behavior and determined the way he ran the affairs of the country when he assumed power on March 25, 1975.

As soon as Faisal was assassinated, Khalid became the next king. When Khalid left Faisal's funeral he cried openly in public and had to be supported by Anwar Sadat of Egypt and Yasir Arafat of the Palestine Liberation Organization (PLO). This open display of affection towards his brother reveals much about Khalid.

Little is known about how the Saud family chooses its king, but it is believed that maternal tribal ties play a part in the decision, and a king is chosen from amongst the oldest sons of Abdul Aziz after much discussion and bargaining. If succession naturally fell to the next oldest, Khalid would not have been the rightful successor to the crown. Muhammad bin Abd al-Aziz was older than Khalid and should have been the rightful heir.

Muhammad had a bad reputation and was referred to as Muhammad of the Twin Evils, as he was known as a drunk and a degenerate. The House of Saud was divided at this point. Muhammad's followers wanted him to become king, while Khalid's supporters felt Khalid was the best choice. Muhammad was offered the position of crown prince but turned it down.

In 1978, Muhammad shot his granddaughter to death and beheaded her boyfriend. His granddaughter had dishonored the family by being with her boyfriend, whom she loved. When they were caught they were arrested, and although the granddaughter and young boy hadn't broken any laws, Muhammad took the law into his own hands. This is often referred to as tribal law and not the law of Islam, which says people are allowed a trial. According to tribal law, the father or a male cousin or a grandfather has the right to deliver punishment for disobedience as he sees fit. Muhammad saw killing his granddaughter, a Saud princess, as his right.

Although King Khalid and Prince Fahd tried to intervene on behalf of the princess, Muhammad was determined to see this through and bring honor to his family. Afterward, Khalid and Fahd acted as if nothing had happened and no one dared to bring charges against Muhammad. This caused much controversy in England, where a movie was made about the inhumane treatment of women, even those in the Saudi royal family.

It was probably best that Muhammad was bypassed in favor of Khalid as king. This was confirmed by Faisal himself, who had proclaimed Khalid his successor before he died. He defused two other potential threats in the House of Saud by naming his ambitious sons, Fahd and Abdullah, crown prince and deputy prime minister and commander of the National Guard, respectively. Fahd is Saudi Arabia's present king, and Abdullah is now crown prince.

Khalid was known as the quiet one, and many thought he would not make a good ruler, but he ruled with strength and persistence. He was consistent in his leadership and especially effective during the moments of crisis that arose during his rule. Unlike King Faisal, Khalid was more liberal in the way he governed. He gave more authority to his policy makers, most of whom had worked for King Faisal. He also allowed the governors more power and he informed the press of the rationale behind his policies. Before Khalid, kings didn't feel the need to explain why they passed a law or made a decision about the kingdom's policies.

Khalid kept the people of Saudi Arabia well informed. He opened up the government to the people so that they would know some of what was going on in and with their country. Khalid saw important changes during his reign. The oil boom had started the year before, in 1974, and lasted until 1985. But even with oil and tremendous amounts of money pouring in, he realized that the oil wouldn't last forever and turned his attention to other areas, especially agriculture.

One of Khalid's first accomplishments occurred in April 1975, when he settled debate over ownership of the land between Saudi Arabia, Oman, and Abu Dhabi known as the Al Buraymi Oasis. His reputation as a statesman grew, and people began to have more faith in the quiet king.

King Khalid still faced many of the same problems Faisal had faced. He worked to keep relations between the Arab states strong and to keep the Soviet Union at bay. In 1976, King Khalid visited the Gulf states to promote unity and closer relations with Saudi Arabia's neighbors. These early visits probably helped in the creation of the GCC, the Gulf Cooperation Council.

Khalid suffered from many medical ailments. He had a heart problem and this may have hampered his ability to rule to his fullest extent. He relied on Fahd, who was already involved in foreign affairs and oil policy and had developed the League of Arab States, a peacekeeping force. Khalid had open-heart surgery in Cleveland, Ohio and though it was successful, his health continued to deteriorate.

Developing the agriculture on the peninsula was one of Khalid's most significant domestic accomplishments. Until the late 1970s, although the Bedouin way of life was rapidly diminishing as more people settled near urban areas and worked for wages to make a living, agriculture was not fully developed. The Arabian Peninsula relied too much on imports of produce from other countries. Developing a strong agricultural base would provide not only food, but also jobs for the people of Saudi Arabia. Khalid wanted to modernize and commercialize agriculture. He spent money on the infrastructure, producing electricity and developing irrigation, drainage, and secondary road systems. He established places to market and distribute the produce. Land was given to individuals and to companies, who had to develop 25 percent of it in two to five years in order to win full ownership of the land.

The Ministry of Agriculture and Water, the Saudi Arabian Agricultural Bank (SAAB), and the Grain Silos and Flour Mills Organization (GSFMO) aided in the development of agriculture. SAAB gave farmers interest-free loans, and the GSFMO purchased produce from the farmers.

King Khalid was not immune to crisis. In 1979, Egypt signed a peace treaty with Israel. Khalid, a strong supporter of Arab unity, was opposed to this arrangement and led economic sanctions against Egypt.

In 2000, members of the Gulf Cooperation Council (GCC) met in their annual summit and signed a defense pact, pledging to aid each other in the event of military attack. The six member nations are Saudi Arabia, Kuwait, Qatar, Oman, Bahrain, and the United Arab Emirates.

At this time, a group of 500 dissidents led by a Sunni named Juhaiman bin Muhammad bin Saif Al Utaiba seized the Grand Mosque and claimed the House of Saud had lost its legitimacy through corruption, ostentation, and imitation of the West. Khalid and the royal family were shocked by this

The green circles are crops thriving in the yellow sands of the Saudi desert, thanks to "center-pivot irrigation" methods, which draw water from up to 4,000 feet underground up to the surface. This photo was taken from the space shuttle *Columbia*.

takeover, as the Grand Mosque is considered sacred ground. Khalid and his advisors listened to the complaints of the dissidents and worked to resolve the problems throughout the peninsula that had led to the protest.

During his rule, Khalid established the King Faisal University in Dammam and Ummul Qura. He funded the building of grain silos and flour mills and the kingdom's wheat production exceeded its consumption. He founded the Ministries of Industry and Electricity, built hospitals, and strengthened the Army and National Guard.

King Fahd in September of 1990.

King Fahd

With the blessing and grace of Almighty God and with the assistance of the faithful Saudi people, we shall continue the welfare march of construction and development, and maintain the gains which are reflected by comprehensive achievements in many fields.
KING FAHD

When Khalid died in 1982, there was no doubt who would succeed him on the Saudi throne. Fahd had already been a spokesman for Khalid and gained much exposure and experience. When he became king, he named Abdullah crown prince. The two sons who had always wanted to be rulers now had their turn.

King Fahd is still the ruler of Saudi Arabia today. He is the eldest son of Abdul Aziz and one of his favorite wives, Hussah al-Sudeiri. Abdul Aziz never divorced her, and she also had a lot of influence over the old monarch. She was involved in the upbringing of the sons she bore and taught them to be completely loyal to each other. She also met with her sons weekly to discuss current events and the royal family in general. Her seven sons were often referred to as the Sudeiri Seven. Their loyalty to each other has allowed them positions of power and control in the government. In order of age, they are: Prince Fahd, Prince Sultan, Prince Abdul Rahman, Prince Naif, Prince Turki, Prince Salman, and Prince Ahmed.

King Fahd was born in the palace in Riyadh in 1923. Like the other sons, he received a court education. Unlike his half-brothers, Fahd was too young to join his father in the battles to unify Arabia; he had no military experience. His first government position was Minister of Education under King Faisal. This daunting job required not only the creation of an educational system in a country that had none, but incorporating girls into the educational system, as well. He used the money from oil to build desperately needed schools around the country. Although many universities and schools were being built, the academic standards were very low. Fahd was interested in developing the higher education system and expanding the construction of universities, something he continued even after he became king.

In 1964, Fahd became the Minister of the Interior, a much more influential and politically powerful position than Minister of Education. This promotion was considered his next step toward the throne.

He caught the attention of many people when a group of terrorists attacked oil installations in 1967. Fahd ordered the arrest of anyone suspected of being part of the attack and, when it was thought the terrorists had come from Yemen, he ordered thousands of Yemeni manual laborers deported on the grounds that their presence posed a threat to internal security.

In another case in 1969, a group consisting mostly of army and air force officers planned a coup to oust King Faisal. When their plan was uncovered, Fahd reportedly ordered that those involved be rounded up and executed.

Although Fahd effectively kept the peace in Saudi Arabia, Faisal was growing concerned about Fahd's suitability as the next king. Fahd had a gambling problem. At a hotel in Monte Carlo, many people witnessed the wealthy royal losing more money in one night than most people make in a lifetime. This arrogant and wasteful display damaged his chances of becoming the next king. King Faisal sent a message to Fahd, ordering his immediate return to Riyadh. Although Faisal threatened to disinherit him, Fahd continued gambling. Not only did his flamboyance upset his half-brother Faisal, but Fahd's behavior also broke the Islamic law that bans all gambling.

In the late 1970s, Fahd became the architect of Saudi foreign policy. He was torn between his pro-American leanings, his loyalty to other Arab nations, and his own family. Many Americans had been brought to Saudi Arabia to train the Saudi military, and anti-American countries and even some members of the royal family resented their presence. Fahd, as spokesman for the Saudi government, continually denied the presence of the American military in Saudi Arabia. The irony is that the Saudi government wanted American weapons and aircraft, but its armed forces didn't know how to use them. They could buy all the F-15s they wanted, but who would fly them? Certainly not young Bedouin camel herders. Without the American military training, the jets and weapons would be useless. Fahd knew that he needed the Americans but he also had to keep peace with the anti-American countries and the people.

In 1980, the royal family attempted to distance itself from the United States. At this time, the United States was helping Afghanistan against the Soviet Union. The Soviet Union was backing the Palestinian people against the Israeli, Zionist occupation. The Saudi royal family questioned the United States' rationale for helping the Afghanistan people but not supporting Palestine. At the same time, Saudi Arabia accused the Soviet Union of supporting one Islamic country and attacking another. The Saudi government could not have it both ways. The United States had been an ally to Israel in the past and would be in the future. Fahd realized that he would always have to maintain a fine balance between his pro-American feelings and those who were anti-American. If the United States were to one day completely support the Palestinian people, relations between Saudi Arabia and other Islamic nations would certainly change. However, the United States' loyalty to Israel would remain unchanged for many years to come.

In the late 1970s and 1980s, the royal family made decisions based on two issues: economic self-interest and the need to protect the kingdom from Soviet influence. Because of this, Saudi Arabia takes a moderate stand on oil pricing. If they raise the price of oil, the United States and other countries feel the pressure and buy less, promoting inflation and affecting the economy. Because the royal family's assets are in dollars (not Francs, Marks, or gold) their profits are directly affected by any change in oil prices.

THE REIGN OF FAHD

When Fahd became king, the country had been in the middle of an oil boom that began around 1974, when Khalid was king. In 1982, the average export price per barrel of oil was above $30. The higher oil revenue meant more money for the royal family and thus development and construction in many areas increased. But because there was more oil being processed, a world oil surplus developed and the price per barrel dropped, resulting in a 20 percent drop in oil revenues. They continued to drop until the oil price crash of 1986.

Now Fahd had to deal with the repercussions. Saudi wealth decreased and development around the country slowed down. Much of the developments started by Khalid during the boom became a burden. The high cost to maintain facilities and infrastructure could no longer be supported. The agricultural sector was hit hardest. Saudi Arabia had become self-sufficient in several major food grains, but the cost to do so was unjustified.

King Fahd maintained the ties with Egypt that had been established in 1987. In July of 2000, he met with Egyptian President Hosni Mubarak (left) in Jeddah. The two leaders met for talks on the negotiations over Jerusalem at the Camp David Summit.

Agricultural employment was on the decline and large conglomerates profited instead of the peasant farmers.

The reduction in Saudi wealth did not seem to affect Saudi's influence in the Arab world. Fahd himself became a major mediator in Arab conflicts. In 1989, Fahd helped in efforts to stop the fighting in Lebanon. He brought the entire Lebanese National Assembly, which included both Christian and Muslim deputies, to the Saudi resort city of Taif. The Assembly couldn't meet in Lebanon because of outbreaks in violence between the military and politically motivated groups. Once at Taif, the Assembly was able to negotiate and incorporate a new plan for reform, and elect a new president.

The year 1987 brought important changes with Egypt. The Saudi government re-established ties with Egypt and King Fahd visited that country in March 1989. The people of Cairo greeted him with enthusiasm, perhaps seeing a chance for peace and unity between the two Arab nations. Egypt, the country of Nasser, who had once tried to overthrow King Faisal, was once again welcomed into the Arab community, led by King Fahd himself.

King Fahd also reorganized the government of the Saudi kingdom. On January 3, 1992, he announced the establishment of four new systems: The Basic Government System, The Consultative Council or Majlis Al-Shura Council System, The Provincial System, and The Council of Ministers System.

Because of these new systems, the king and his ministers didn't have complete and total rule over the government or the country anymore. There were limitations that had never been implemented before, and some checks and balances. The State's legislative and executive authorities would be limited to specific terms, after which membership would be renewed or new members appointed for four-year terms.

The aim of the new systems was to tap the pool of qualified youths in the country. Fahd had noticed that much talent and intelligence was going unused in Saudi Arabia. Many young Saudi men and women were being educated outside of Saudi Arabia and their experience and knowledge could be a tremendous resource to the Saudi government.

The Basic Law of Government confirms that the system of government in the kingdom of Saudi Arabia is a monarchy. The Basic System establishes the general principles on which the kingdom of Saudi Arabia was founded. Article 1 clearly establishes the central tenets of the kingdom and has not swayed from the original beliefs laid down by Abdul Aziz when he first formed the united Saudi Arabia in 1932. Article 1 states: The Kingdom of Saudi Arabia is an Arab and Islamic Sovereign State; its religion is Islam and its constitution is the Holy Koran and the Prophet's Sunnah. Its language is Arabic and its capital is Riyadh.

The Basic Law gives power to the sons of the Founder, King Abdul Aziz Al Saud, and their offspring, and shall go to those who are most qualified. The king presides over the Council of Ministers, which controls the executive and organizational powers. Currently, the Council is composed of two deputy premiers and twenty-two ministers. They run the affairs of state in the sovereignty, services, and development sectors.

The sovereignty sector includes the Interior, Foreign, Defense, and Justice Ministries.

The services sector includes the Ministries of Health, Education, Higher Education, Communications, PTT, Public Works and Housing, Labor and Social Affairs, Hajj, Islamic Affairs, Dawa and Endowments, Information, and Municipal and Rural Affairs.

The development sector includes the Ministries of Finance, Commerce, Planning, Agriculture and Water, Industry and Electricity, and Petroleum and Mineral Resources.

Linked to these ministries are several public agencies.

The kingdom has thirteen regions controlled by local governors, all appointed by the king. Each governor acts in the same way as the governors of the states in the United States. Although it is similar in some areas to the kind of democracy we are used to in the United States, the Saudi government is quick to point out that the Saudi system of government, as defined under the Basic System and the establishment of the Consultative Council, is not a move towards Western-style democracy, much less an imitation of Western-style democratic reform. It is a development of the relationship between the leader and the people that is part of Islamic tradition.

The Consultative Council, or Majlis Al-Shura, formalized the people's participation in government in Saudi Arabia. The Majlis had already existed in the region for many centuries. Abdul Aziz and the kings after him all used this important aspect of Saudi governing. It allows the citizens of Saudi Arabia to air their grievances, complaints, needs, and suggestions to the king or a minister. The establishment of the Council marked the first steps towards a more formal, broadly based involvement of the people in the kingdom's political processes.

The Consultative Council consists of a speaker and sixty members selected by the king. In 2001, the number of members grew to 120. Members of the Council are also able to review legislation and domestic and foreign policies.

King Fahd's desire to increase the pace of modernization while remaining firmly within the religious and cultural traditions of the kingdom seems to be working.

KING FAHD'S FOREIGN POLICY

One of the goals of King Fahd and his ministry is to bring about unity among the Arab countries of the Middle East. Just like his father and brothers before him, he realizes the importance of uniting the countries of Islam. Separately, they are not strong; little good has come of their fighting with each other. The ultimate objective of King Fahd is a realistic peace. There must be compromise and negotiation and the end result should be fair to both sides. His position on the Palestinian and Israeli conflict reflects this view.

THE PALESTINIAN-ISRAELI PROBLEM

After World War II and the vicious attack on Jews by Nazi Germany, millions of displaced Jews found themselves without a country, with no place to live or call home. They were sent to the land of Palestine, now Israel. Palestine was not an empty space waiting to be filled. It was the home of the Palestinian people. As the Jews were sent in, the Palestinian people were uprooted and displaced. Countries such as the United States and Europe supported the Jewish occupation of Palestine; after all, it was also considered their homeland and seemed to be a reasonable place to go. There were already Jews living in Palestine, but there were half again as many Arabs as Jews.

Many Arabs viewed this as racial cleansing. Palestinians were forced to leave their homes and businesses and herded into small areas or kept at refugee camps. Both sides felt the land was theirs

In 1948, Arab refugees fled to Lebanon to escape the Arab-Israeli War being fought in the Galilee region in northern Israel, formerly a part of Palestine. The Arabs claim that the land occupied by Israel was given to them by God through Abraham's son Ishmael. Ishmael was the son of Abraham and Hagar—who, according to tradition, was the daughter of an Egyptian pharaoh—and is considered the ancestor of the Arabs by both Muslims and Jews. The Jews claim that God gave them Israel through Abraham's son Isaac, born of Sarai (Sarah) and considered the ancestor of the Jewish people.

and called on the same story in the Old Testament, the story about Abraham, as evidence that God gave them the land. The Jews claimed the land was passed to them from Abraham through his son, Isaac. The Palestinians claimed the land was passed to them through his other son, Ishmael. Both sides have attacked each other and both are guilty of terrorism and inhumane acts.

What seems to confuse the Saudi kings is how the West can sympathize with one group of persecuted people, the Jews, and not show the same sympathy for another group of persecuted people, the Palestinians. If it was wrong for the Nazis to deny the rights of citizenship to the Jews, it must surely be wrong for

Israel to deny the rights of citizenship to the Palestinians; if it was wrong for the Nazis to use the military power of the State to oppress a people, it must be wrong for the Israelis to oppress the Palestinians. If it was wrong for the Nazis to arrest Jews without due process of law, it must be wrong for the Israelis to carry out mass arrests of Palestinians without due legal process.

King Fahd has always supported Palestine, just as his father did. He planned to bring about peace in the region. In August 1981, Crown Prince Fahd created an eight-point peace plan. The points of the Fahd Plan were

1. that Israel would withdraw from all Arab territory occupied in 1967, including Arab Jerusalem;
2. that Israeli settlements built on Arab land after 1967 would be dismantled, including those in Arab Jerusalem;
3. that freedom of worship would be guaranteed for all religions in the Holy Places;
4. that the Palestinian Arab people would have the right to return to their homes, and that those who did not wish to return would be compensated;
5. that the West Bank and the Gaza Strip would have a transitional period, administered by the United Nations, for a period not exceeding a few months;
6. that an independent Palestinian state would be established, with Jerusalem as its capital city;
7. that all states in the region *should* be able to live in peace; and
8. that the United Nations or member states of the United Nations would guarantee the carrying out of these provisions.

The Fahd Plan was significant in several ways. First, it showed that the kingdom of Saudi Arabia was prepared to take the initiative in trying to solve the problems posed by Israel. Second, it indicated the type of approach King Fahd would take to international diplomacy.

Many Arab nations did not like Fahd's plan because it gave the Jewish state a right to exist alongside a Palestinian state. Today, however, despite all the efforts of King Fahd and several other countries including the United States, conflict between the Jews and Arabs is at an all-time high. The problem lies not with the average person of each nation, but with the extremists who use terrorism as their weapon, hurting and killing innocent people. Until they are gone, the peace process can't continue. In the meantime, Saudi Arabia continues to support the Palestinians in many ways.

THE GULF WAR

Iraq declared victory over Iran after the Iraq-Iran War in 1988, but was economically hurt in the process. Hoping to regain stability through oil sales, Iraq's president, Saddam Hussein, became angry when Kuwait and the United Arab Emirates exceeded their OPEC quotas. Desperate to rebuild his economy, Hussein aggressively attacked Kuwait first by demanding that all of Iraq's war debts be cancelled, and then by accusing Kuwait of stealing $2.4 billion worth of oil from an Iraqi oil field.

Because Saudi Arabia had backed Iraq against Iran, Iraq was sure that they would do the same in their efforts against Kuwait. When an attempt was made to resolve the problem, it became clear that Kuwait could not meet Saddam Hussein's demands. Saddam Hussein promised King Fahd that he would not invade Kuwait. When he went back on his word, it came as a shock to King Fahd.

On August 2, 1990, Saddam Hussein gained control of Kuwait. The United Nations condemned Iraq, and Saudi Arabia immediately sent troops to its borders. In Cairo, The Arab League also condemned Iraq. On August 12, Hussein announced that if Israel withdrew from Palestine, he would withdraw from Kuwait. Arab nations saw a similarity between what Iraq was doing in Kuwait and what Israel was doing in the occupation of Palestine. This explains why Iraq later sent scud missiles to bomb Israel.

U.S. troops deploy across the Saudi desert on November 4, 1990, preparing to liberate Kuwait from Iraq in Desert Storm.

Atrocities committed by Iraqi troops against the Kuwaiti people were relayed to King Fahd and the rest of the world. It became urgent that Saudi Arabia attempt to liberate Kuwait. In order to do this, Saudi Arabia would need the power and might of a bigger country—the United States. To ensure that the alliance was acting within United Nations authority, on November 29 the United States drafted a resolution declaring that if Iraq had not fully complied with earlier United Nations resolutions demanding its withdrawal from Kuwait by January 15, 1991, the alliance could use "all necessary means" to ensure compliance. This resolution (No. 678) was adopted by the United Nations.

In the middle of January, Desert Storm began. Air assaults bombarded Iraq. In late January, Iraqi troops invaded a deserted town over the Saudi border but they were quickly repelled by Saudi troops. The alliance between Saudi Arabia, the United States, and other countries angered Hussein and he retaliated by sending scud missiles to Saudi Arabia. His main objective was the capital city of Riyadh, though most missiles never hit their intended target. The war itself was over before it even began. Although Iraq did much damage to Kuwait's oil fields, the alliance against Iraq nearly wiped out Iraq's army.

Many in the Arab world view King Fahd's reliance on the United States as dangerous. Since the Gulf War, American troops have inhabited parts of Saudi Arabia and Bahrain, something that greatly upsets anti-American Arab countries. But Saudi Arabia could not have expelled Iraq from Kuwait without the help of the United States and the alliance it formed with western European countries, England, and Canada.

Today, King Fahd faces greater challenges created when terrorists attacked the United States on September 11, turning the world upside down. With Fahd's health failing and another king in the waiting, Saudi Arabia may be in for yet another dramatic change. The future is never certain, and how the Saudi government and the royal family conduct themselves in foreign policy could help them or destroy them. Today, the family is still wealthy and powerful and still must maintain its relationship with the United States as well as other Arab nations. What will the future hold for Saudi Arabia, and what questions have current events raised in the minds of many Americans and freedom-loving countries around the world?

Saudi Arabia's foreign minister, Prince Saud bin Faisal bin Abd al-Aziz Al Saud (Prince Saud al-Faisal), met with President Bush in Washington on September 20, 2001, before Bush announced his administration's plans to fight terrorism.

8

Friend or Foe: The Future of Saudi Arabia

Since the terrorist attack on the United States on September 11, 2001, the world has changed in many ways. The relationships among Saudi Arabia, its royal family, and the United States are continually being tested. Saudi Arabia, situated geographically in the midst of other Arab nations, finds itself torn between keeping Arab unity and taking a stronger stand against terrorism. In the past, Saudi Arabia and the royal family have tried to keep the peace while maintaining this quest for unity and keeping the country independent from countries like the United States.

The Gulf War proved that Saudi Arabia depends on the United States as an ally just as much as the United States depends on the continual supply of oil at low prices—if not more. Perhaps the royal family realizes this and is taking "baby steps" in allying itself more with the United States against terrorism and against nations that sponsor terrorist groups. These nations include several Arab nations, such as Palestine, Syria, and Yemen.

In the months following the attack of September 11, against the United States, in which nineteen of the twenty terrorists were from Saudi Arabia, the royal family and its ministry have been scrambling to keep ties open with the United States. On October 4, 2001, Prince Sultan met with U.S. Defense Secretary Donald Rumsfeld and stressed that the friendly ties with the U.S. should remain intact. He denounced the actions of bin Laden and Al Qaeda: "[B]in Laden has shown himself to be a terrorist and a criminal. Bin Laden is not a Saud citizen, and he does not represent the Kingdom of Saudi Arabia."

Problems arise when the royal family says things that seem to encourage peace and prosperity between the two nations but doesn't act on them; the United States is finding this among the most frustrating aspects of the fight against terrorism.

Many questions are asked today about the country of Saudi Arabia and its survival. What will happen when the oil is gone and with it goes the kingdom's wealth? How will Saudi Arabia react to other Arab nations who sponsor terrorist groups? Currently, the royal family has said much about the war against terrorism, but its actions don't back what it says. Is the family taking a neutral stand and acting as if nothing happened, as it has in the past? At the time of the writing of this book, the family still has not stopped the flow of money to groups that are believed to have terrorist associations. Nor has it sent its own military to wipe out terrorism.

The royal family, being the sole government of Saudi Arabia, monitors everything that is said about it and the country. Ask a Saudi resident how he feels about his government and the royal family and he will probably tell you that it is fine, that he likes the royal family. If he doesn't have a positive reply, he could be imprisoned. In Saudi jails, prisoners are often tortured before they are found guilty of anything. Saudi citizens often find it best to say only good things about their country, rather than to risk imprisonment.

It would seem that the family members are not only afraid of losing their hold on the oil industry, but also on the people of their country. The senior princes don't allow political expression, particularly if it is negative. They developed SANG, the Saudi Arabia National Guard, whose sole purpose is to protect the royal family from a takeover. No one quite knows how many men are part of SANG, but it is estimated that the small army numbers between 50,000 and 100,000 men. Why would the royal family need so many bodyguards if it didn't feel threatened? Is the royal family trying to keep the peace in its own country by not becoming more involved with the United States and its war on terror? As in many Arab nations, there is anti-American sentiment in Saudi Arabia. Many Arabs wish to see Israel become a Palestinian state and perhaps there won't be any action until the United States encourages Israel to back off.

Members of the royal family are not only torn in their loyalties to each other, the oil industry, and Islam; the country itself and its people are also torn. Because of the wealth created by the oil industry, there is now a middle class in Saudi Arabia. This class of people is educated. More young Saudis are being educated in the United States and experiencing firsthand the Western lifestyle—freedom of speech, the freedom to worship as they choose, and the freedom to disagree with the government. In Saudi Arabia, this middle class is becoming more discontented with the royal family. The royal family cannot control all negative press about it, especially in other countries. Many Saudis are discovering unpleasant truths about the royal family, in particular its corruption and illegal activities.

Many Saudis are not willing to work, either; not when the money from the oil industry flows in so abundantly. They want a piece of this industry and, in some ways, feel they deserve it without having to work for it. The labor force in Saudi Arabia consists mostly of foreigners. They dig the ditches, pick up the trash, and drive the buses; all are jobs that many native Saudis feel are beneath them or simply won't do. Students at universities

Afghani workers in Riyadh in 2001. Thousands of people born in Afghanistan work as laborers in Saudi Arabia. In 2001, the population of Saudi Arabia exceeded 22.1 million; of this number, 74% are Saudi citizens and 26% non-Saudis. Of the workforce of 7.2 million, 56% are non-Saudis.

see themselves becoming businessmen and women. This means they'd like to become partners with companies outside the kingdom. The only way a foreigner can enter the kingdom is through an employer who sponsors him or her. Saudi Arabia does not allow tourist visas. These students see themselves becoming agents, getting the workers from overseas companies along with the profits.

The royal family, especially the senior princes, tend to side with isolationism. They feel safer keeping the West in the west and isolating their citizens from outside influences. When foreigners are in the country, they may not associate with Saudi nationals. Their living quarters are separate and they are kept away from Saudi citizens. The non-Western foreign workers often live and work on the job site and are exploited so badly that it is very hard for them to ever break their contract with a company. They are often forced to work until death.

As hard as Saudi Arabia tries to be modern, true modernity is a way of thinking, not a way to construct buildings or do business with other modern countries.

The royal family is constantly under attack. The senior princes, including the sons of Abdul Aziz bin Saud, were raised in a time when Saudi Arabia was more isolated from the rest of the world. Their sons and grandsons are living in today's world. While preaching the Koran and Islamic law in one breath, some members of the royal family break laws, oppress their subjects, and act in opposition to their stated beliefs. Saudi citizens don't need Western newspapers and magazines to see this. It's happening in front of them, in their own country. Despite the royal family's tremendous wealth, poverty in Saudi Arabia is still evident. The royal family spends millions on luxurious palaces while some citizens are hungry and homeless.

Many students blame the royal family for the country's "backwardness." Students today will be tomorrow's business-men and women, leaders with families of their own. The royal family seems ill-prepared to deal with the future dissidence that is inevitable.

RELIGIOUS EXTREMISM AND SAUDI ARABIA

Some may say that the threat of religious extremism is nonexistent in Saudi Arabia because the country already practices a stricter form of Islam than any other country in the world. However, one of the greatest threats to the House of Al Saud is that the family has no religious legitimacy as a ruling body. In Islam, hereditary power is forbidden. Some scholars of the Koran say that Islam calls for a democracy, complete with elections—not the current monarchial state held by the House of Saud. Because the ruling family is so closely tied to Islam, many see this relationship as an injustice to Islam. After all, the royal family has not always practiced what it preached.

As with the Bible, people interpret the Koran in different ways. These interpretations are seen as a threat to the royal family. Some claim that the Koran says things such as "consultation with the people in the affairs of state," while the royal family interprets these things differently, or perhaps ignores them altogether. The family's most dangerous enemies are the religious extremists who speak their minds and revolt against the system and the Saudi regime.

Today, religious extremists are found all over the world. Islam, Christianity, and other religions all have members who see things quite differently. Saudi Arabia has groups of extremists living inside and outside its borders. Many questions have developed since the 2001 terrorist attacks on the United States. Nineteen of the twenty terrorists were Saudi nationals trained by Al Qaeda, which was led by Osama bin Laden, also a Saudi national who was stripped of his citizenship in 1994. Despite this, links between Osama and Saudi Arabia are still evident. Although the ambassador to the United States has clearly stated the Saudi position against Osama bin Laden and the terrorist group, Al Qaeda, Saudi Arabia is not acting on those words.

We do know that these men were part of an extremist group who practiced a different kind of Islam. These terrorists also pose a threat to Saudi Arabia. The royal family could be a possible target of terrorism in the future.

Since bin Laden was deprived of his citizenship, his main goal has been to overthrow the Saudi government—the government that he believes preaches the most conservative Islam in the world, yet is full of corruption and allies itself with the United States and allows the U.S. military on its sacred land. The royal family fears bin Laden and his group of extremists and this may explain its hesitation in acting against them.

Internal discontent, a war on terrorism, extremist religious leaders, dwindling oil, Western ways and values, corruption,

Osama bin Laden, whose Saudi citizenship was revoked in 1994, is the prime suspect in the 2001 terrorist attack on the United States. This photograph was taken in 1998 in Afghanistan.

jealousy among family members, and a general uncertainty have plagued the House of Saud in more recent times. Finding a balance between wealth and Islamic faith has been hard, if not impossible.

Saudi Arabia is the only country in the world that has seen such incredible change and rapid growth in such a short period of time. Saudi Arabia remains an introverted society with a

Crown Prince Abdullah (center), son of King Abdul Aziz, and Foreign Minister Prince Saud al-Faisal (left) at the 2001 summit of the GCC in Muscat, Oman. Despite its progress in uniting the Arab nations, Saudi Arabia remains an introverted society, practicing the strict form of Islam dictated by the Wahhabi sect. Elsewhere in the Arab world, Muslim women don't completely cover their faces.

government system headed by aged and ailing members of the royal family. Saudi Arabia's friendship, more a convenient business deal, with the United States has so far survived despite Saudi Arabia's lack of democracy or accountability and its intense Islamic conservatism. But relations have been tested by terrorism. The very survival of the Saudi regime is at stake on many different levels.

King Fahd's health has been deteriorating since a series of strokes in the late 1990s. Crown Prince Abdullah has been handling much of the kingdom's policies, but the throne may not automatically go to the prince in the event of King Fahd's death. The King's two full brothers, Defense Minister Prince Sultan and Interior Minister Prince Nayef—half-brothers of the Crown Prince—are also contenders. Crown Prince Abdullah stands firm in his position on Palestine, but surprised many in the Arab world in an interview with the German magazine *Der Spiegel*. He said, "For more than fifty years, no Arab had thought that it was possible to live together with Israel. Today we have arrived at the point where Arabs and Israelis can begin a new life together. We have a real chance for peace." His position does not agree with many in the Arab world. Statements like this could damage his chances of becoming the next king.

And then there is the oil industry, which won't be around forever. If the royal family does not continue to develop other industries and agriculture, then when the oil is gone Saudi Arabia as we know it today will also disappear.

The ideas Abdul Aziz once had for his united Arabia seem to be long forgotten. The discovery of oil has changed the country forever, from its leaders down to its common citizens. Discontent and frustration hover over the House of Saud as it tries to make peace within its own confines, with its people, and with the countries of the world.

Despite its corruption and seemingly backward ways, the Saudi royal family has improved the overall well-being of its citizens by building schools and hospitals and incorporating some modern ways into Saudi society. As in any family, some members are more productive than others. Some have big hearts and grand ideas while others can't seem to do anything right. Like everyone on earth, members of the royal family are only human despite the vast riches they possess. With this humanity come many imperfections.

What the future holds for Saudi Arabia is hard to tell. What the future holds for the House of Saud, the richest family in the world, only its members can determine.

Al Saud — Literally, the House of Saud; the patrilineal descendants of Muhammad bin Saud.

emir — (amir) Strictly speaking, commander. In Saudi Arabia, *emir* often means prince, but it can designate the governor of a province.

barrels per day (bpd) — Production of crude oil and petroleum products is frequently measured in barrels per day, often abbreviated as *bpd*. A barrel is a volume measure of 42 U.S. gallons. Conversion of barrels to tons depends on the density of the specific product. About 17.3 barrels of average crude oil is equal in weight to one ton. Light products, such as gasoline and kerosene, would average close to eight barrels per ton.

Ikhwan — The brotherhood of desert warriors, founded by Abdul Aziz bin Saud.

majlis — Tribal council. In some countries, the legislative assembly. Also the audience of the king, emir, or shaykh, open to all citizens for the purposes of adjudication.

riyal (SR or SAR) — Saudi Arabia's unit of currency. In May of 1993, the exchange rate was SR3.75 = US$1, a rate that had not changed since June 1, 1986; at the time of the writing of this book, the rate of exchange was approximately the same: a riyal was equal in value to US$0.26 or US$0.27.

Sharia — The Islamic religious, social, and political law—in general, the foundation of Islamic thought, influenced by many religious and historical sources, including especially the Koran. The Sharia can apply very much or not much at all, depending on the situation. It often governs marriage and inheritance.

sharif (s.), *ashraf (pl.)* — Specifically, one who is descended from Muhammad through his daughter Fatima. Literally, noble, exalted, having descent from illustrious ancestors. Frequently used as an honorific title.

shaykh/shiekh — Leader or chief. Applied either to political leaders of tribes or towns or learned religious leaders. Also used as an honorific.

Sunni — The larger of the two great divisions of Islam. The Sunni, who rejected the claims of Ali's line, believe that they are the true followers of the Sunna, the guide to proper behavior set forth by Muhammad's personal deeds and sayings.

Wahhabi — Name used outside of Saudi Arabia to designate followers of Wahhabism.

Wahhabism — Name used outside of Saudi Arabia to designate the official interpretation of Islam in Saudi Arabia. The faith is a very conservative version of unitarianism, the call to oneness or unity with God (*ad dawa lil tawhid*), that was preached by Muhammad bin Abd al-Wahhab. His Muslim opponents named his philosophy after its leader.

GEOGRAPHICAL NAMES

The Hijaz and Asir — Two mountainous areas on the western coast of Saudi Arabia near Mecca and Medina. There are virtually no natural harbors on the Red Sea where these mountain ranges meet the coast.

Najd (Nejd) — A rocky plateau east of the Hijaz and Asir, with small deserts and mountains. This area is home to the pastoral Shammar tribes, who, led by the Al Rashid, were the enemies of the Al Saud in the late 19th and early 20th centuries. Their capital was the large oasis of Hail, now a flourishing urban center.

Northern Arabia (Badiyat ash Sham) — An upland plateau, geographically part of the Syrian Desert, with numerous wadis (riverbeds), most winding northeast toward Iraq. This area is covered with grass and scrub vegetation and is used as a pasture by nomadic and semi-nomadic herders.

Eastern Arabia (Al Hasa) — Contains the largest oasis in the country. Meets the Persian Gulf and has an irregular coastline with sandy plains, marshes, and salt flats.

The Great Deserts — Three great deserts isolate Najd from the north, east, and south. In the north, the An Nafud—sometimes called the Great Nafud because An Nafud is the term for desert—covers about 55,000 square kilometers. Ad Dahna is a narrow band of sand mountains also called the river of sand. Rub al Khali, one of the truly forbidding sand deserts in the world and, until the 1950s, one of the least explored.

1720–1725	Saud bin Muhammad bin Mugrin
1725–1765	Muhammad bin Saud
1765–1803	Abdul Aziz bin Muhammad
1788–1813	Saud bin Abd al-Aziz
1813–1818	Abdullah bin Saud
1818–1820	Mishari bin Saud & Muhammad bin Mishari bin Mu'amar—fought for leadership for 18 months during the Egyptian occupation.
1820–1830	Turki bin Abdullah bin Saud
1830	Mishari bin Abdullah bin Hassan bin Mishari bin Saud
1830–1839	Faisal bin Turki (first rule)
1839–1841	Khalid bin Saud bin Abd al-Aziz
1841–1842	Abdullah bin Thunaiyan bin Saud
1842–1865	Faisal bin Turki (second rule)
1865–1874	Abdullah bin Faisal and Saud bin Faisal—fought for leadership for nine years
1874–1884	Abdullah bin Faisal
1884–1889	Occupation and rule by the Rashid family
1889–1890	Abdul Rahman bin Faisal
1891–1901	Occupation and rule by the Rashid family
1901–1953	Abdul Aziz bin Abd al-Rahman
1953–1964	Saud bin Abd al-Aziz
1964–1975	Faisal bin Abd al-Aziz
1975–1982	Khalid bin Abd al-Aziz
1982–present	Fahd bin Abd al-Aziz
Heir	Crown Prince Abdullah bin Abd al-Aziz Al Saud

1871	The Ottoman Empire takes control of the province of Hasa.
1880	Abdul Aziz Al Saud is born in Riyadh.
1891	The Al Saud family is exiled to Kuwait by the Rashid family.
1902	Abdul Aziz Al Saud takes control of Riyadh, bringing the Al Saud family back into Saudi Arabia.
1912	Abdul Aziz Al Saud founds the Ikhwan (Brotherhood).
1913	Abdul Aziz Al Saud takes Hasa from the Ottoman Empire.
1921	Abdul Aziz Al Saud takes the title Sultan of Najd.
1924	Mecca regained.
1925	Medina retaken.
1926	Abdul Aziz is proclaimed King of the Hijaz in the Grand Mosque of Mecca.
1928-30	The Ikhwan turn against Abdul Aziz Al Saud but are defeated by Abdul Aziz Al Saud.
1932	
September	The areas controlled by Abdul Aziz are unified under the name Kingdom of Saudi Arabia, and Abdul Aziz is proclaimed King.
1933	King Abdul Aziz's eldest son, Saud, is named Crown Prince.
1938	Oil is discovered and production begins under the U.S.-controlled ARAMCO (Arabian-American Oil Company).
1953	
November	King Abdul Aziz Al Saud dies and is succeeded by the Crown Prince Saud bin Abd al-Aziz Al Saud. The new King's brother, Faisal is named Crown Prince.
1960	Saudi Arabia is a founding member of OPEC (the Organization of Petroleum-Exporting Countries).
1964	
November	King Saud is deposed by his brother, the Crown Prince, Faisal bin Abd al-Aziz Al Saud.
1970	The OIC (Organization of the Islamic Conference) is founded in Jeddah, Saudi Arabia.
1972	For the first time, Saudi Arabia gains control of a proportion (20%) of ARAMCO, lessening the control of the Americans over Saudi oil.

1973   Saudi Arabia leads an oil boycott against the Western countries that supported Israel in the October War against Egypt and Syria leading to the quadrupling of oil prices.

1975

March   King Faisal is assassinated by his nephew, Faisal bin Musaid bin Abd al-Aziz Al Saud; He is succeeded by his brother, Khalid bin Abd al-Aziz Al Saud.

1979   Saudi Arabia severs diplomatic relations with Egypt after it makes peace with Israel.

1979   Extremists seize the Grand Mosque of Mecca; the government regains control after 10 days and executes those captured.

1980   Saudi Arabia takes full control of ARAMCO from the U.S.

1981

May   Saudi Arabia is a founding member of the GCC (Gulf Cooperation Council).

1982

June   King Khalid dies of a heart attack and is succeeded by his brother, Crown Prince Fahd bin Abd al-Aziz Al Saud.

1986

November   King Fahd adds the title "Custodian of the Two Holy Mosques" to his name.

1987   Saudi Arabia resumes diplomatic relations with Egypt (severed since 1979).

1990   Saudi Arabia condemns the Iraqi invasion of Kuwait and asks the U.S. to intervene; it allows foreign troops, the Kuwaiti government and many of its citizens to stay in Saudi Arabia but expels citizens of Yemen and Jordan due to their governments' support of Iraq.

1991   Saudi Arabia is involved in both air attacks on Iraq and in the land force that went on to liberate Kuwait.

1992

March   King Fahd announces the "Basic System of Government" emphasizing the duties and responsibilities a ruler has for his people and proposed the setting up of a Consultative Council (*majlis al-shura*).

1993

September   King Fahd decrees the division of Saudi Arabia into thirteen administrative divisions.

1993

December The Consultative Council (*majlis al-shura*) is inaugurated. It is composed of a chairman and sixty members chosen by the King.

1994 Islamic dissident Osama bin Laden is stripped of his Saudi nationality.

1995

November King Fahd has a stroke; the daily operations of the country are entrusted to Crown Prince Abdullah bin Abd al-Aziz Al Saud.

1996

February King Fahd resumes control of state affairs.

1996

June A bomb explodes at the U.S. military complex near Dhahran killing 19 and wounding over 300.

1997

July King Fahd increases the members of the Consultative Council (majlis al-shura) from 60 to 90.

1999

October For the first time, twenty Saudi women attend the session of the Consultative Council (majlis al-shura) for the first time.

2000

September The London-based human rights group Amnesty International describes Saudi Arabia's treatment of women, particularly foreign domestic workers, as "untenable" by any legal or moral standard.

2001

April Saudi Arabia and Iran sign a major security accord to combat terrorism, the drug trade, and organized crime.

September Osama bin Laden, a former Saudi national, is accused of launching massive terrorist attacks on the United States. Nineteen of the twenty terrorists involved are also from Saudi Arabia.

October Saudi Family attempts to donate $10 million to relief efforts in New York City. Mayor Rudolph Giuliani does not accept the money.

Aburish, Said K. *The Rise, Corruption, and Coming Fall of the House of Saud.* New York: St. Martin's Press, 1996.

Armstrong, Harold Courtenay. *Lord of Arabia, Ibn Saud: An Intimate Study of a King.* Glen Echo, Maryland: Simon, 2001.

Ellis, Phyllis. *Desert Governess: An Englishwoman's Personal Experience with the Saudi Royal Family.* Travellers Eye, 2000.

Harper, Robert. *Major World Nations: Saudi Arabia.* Philadelphia: Chelsea House, 2002.

Ibrahim, Nasser. *King Fahd and Saudi Arabia's Great Evolution.* Joplin, Missouri: International Institute of Technology, 1987.

Lawrence, T.E. *Seven Pillars of Wisdom: A Triumph.* Homer, Alaska: Anchor, 1991 (Reissue edition).

Sander, Nestor. *Ibn Saud: King by Conquest.* Hats Off, 2001.

Sasson, Jean P. *Princess: A True Story of Life Behind the Veil in Saudi Arabia.* Windsor-Broke, 2001.

Vasilev, A.M. *The History of Saudi Arabia.* New York University Press, 2000.

WEBSITES

Saudi Royal Family Database
www.saudiroyals.com/home.asp

The Saudi Royal Family Directory
www.datarabia.com/royals/default.asp

The Royal Embassy of Saudi Arabia (Washington, D.C.)
www.saudiembassy.net

Saudi Arabia Information Resource
www.saudinf.com/index.htm

The Saudi Network: The Saudi Dynasty
www.the-saudi.net/al-saud/

ArabNet: Saudi, Contents
www.arab.net/saudi/saudi_contents.html

Saudi Strategies: The Al Saud Dynasty
www.saudistrategies.com/alsaud.html

Ajami, Foud. *The Dream Palace of the Arabs.* New York: Pantheon Books 1998.

Anderson, Laurie Halse. *Saudi Arabia.* Minneapolis: Carolrhoda, 2001.

Balcavage, Denise. *Saudi Arabia.* Milwaukee: Garth Stevens, 2001.

The Cambridge Encyclopedia of the Middle East. New York: Cambridge University Press, 1988.

Fazio, Wende. *Saudi Arabia.* New York: Children's Press, 1999.

Fisher, Sidney Nettleton. *The Middle East.* New York: McGraw Hill, 1990.

Goldschmidt, Arthur, Jr. *A Concise History of the Middle East.* Boulder: Westview Press, 1991.

Holden, David, and Richard Johns. *The House of Saud: The Rise and Rule of the Most Powerful Dynasty in the Arab World.* New York: Holt, Rinehart, & Winston, 1981.

Janin, Hunt. *Cultures of the World: Saudi Arabia.* New York: Marshall Cavendish, 1993.

Lewis, Bernard. *The Middle East.* New York: Simon & Schuster, 1995.

McCarthy, Kevin. *Saudi Arabia: A Desert Kingdom.* New Jersey: Dillon Press, 1997.

Powell, William. *Saudi Arabia and Its Royal Family.* Secaucus, New Jersey: Lyle Stuart, 1982.

page:

2: AP/Wide World Photos
11: 21st Century Publishing
12: AP/Wide World Photos
17: Bettmann/Corbis
18: AP/Wide World Photos
21: Wolfgang Kaehler/Corbis
24: AP/Wide World Photos
27: AP/Wide World Photos
31: Bettmann/Corbis
34: AP/Wide World Photos
37: Corbis
41: Bettmann/Corbis
43: AP/Wide World Photos
44: AP/Wide World Photos
46: AP/Wide World Photos
49: AP/Wide World Photos
52: Hulton/Archive by Getty Images

54: Bettmann/Corbis
57: Bettmann/Corbis
60: Corbis
64: AP/Wide World Photos
65: AP/Wide World Photos
66: AP/Wide World Photos
71: AP/Wide World Photos
72: Digital Image © 1996 Corbis: Original images courtesy of NASA/Corbis
74: AP/Wide World Photos
79: AFP/NMI
83: AP/Wide World Photos
86: AP/Wide World Photos
88: AP/Wide World Photos
92: AP/Wide World Photos
95: AP/Wide World Photos
96: AP/Wide World Photos

Cover: Associated Press, AP

JENNIFER BOND REED began writing children's stories as a child for her fourth-grade class; little did she know she'd make a career of it. This is her second book for Chelsea House, and she has sold over 100 stories and articles to children's magazines. Jennifer is also the editor of the e-magazine *Wee Ones* and an instructor for the Institute of Children's Literature. She writes picture-book stories for StoryPlus.com and frequently gives talks and interviews on writing for children and the children's magazine and book industry. She lives in Maryland with her husband, Jeff, and two children, Eric and Emma.

ARTHUR M. SCHLESINGER, jr. is the leading American historian of our time. He won the Pulitzer Prize for his book *The Age of Jackson* (1945) and again for a chronicle of the Kennedy Administration, *A Thousand Days* (1965), which also won the National Book Award. Professor Schlesinger is the Albert Schweitzer Professor of the Humanities at the City University of New York and has been involved in several other Chelsea House projects, including the series REVOLUTIONARY WAR LEADERS, COLONIAL LEADERS, and YOUR GOVERNMENT.